THE BUZZARD

THE BUZZARD

Colin R. Tubbs

DAVID & CHARLES
NEWTON ABBOT LONDON
NORTH POMFRET (VT) VANCOUVER

0 7153 6323 9

Library of Congress Catalog Card Number 74-78245

Set in 12pt Bembo, 1pt leaded and printed in Great Britain by Latimer Trend & Company Ltd Plymouth for David & Charles (Holdings) Limited South Devon House Newton Abbot Devon

Published in the United States of America by David & Charles Inc North Pomfret Vermont 05053 USA

Published in Canada by Douglas David & Charles Limited 3645 McKechnie Drive West Vancouver BC

CONTENTS

LIST OF ILLUSTRATIONS

PLATES

FIGURES

TABLES

INTRODUCTION

Buzzards, circling and calling high up in a cumulus-studded sky, or perched phlegmatically on roadside telegraph poles, are a familiar enough sight in parts of western Britain; nevertheless it comes as something of a surprise to find that the buzzard is one of the most numerous birds of prey in the country. In much of Wales, in south-west England, and in parts of the Scottish Highlands, it is the commonest raptor (that is, a predatory bird equipped with talons), though in the country as a whole there are almost certainly more kestrels and, perhaps, also more sparrowhawks.

Buzzards weigh between 800 and 1,200g and have a wingspan of between 113 and 137cm—the females are larger than the males, as with most raptors. They are thus comparatively large birds. Thought about in terms of live weight, and thus prey requirements, one buzzard would be equal to at least four kestrels, though the validity of such a comparison may be doubtful because the two species do not feed on exactly the same things.

On the wing, the buzzard is unmistakable—a master of thermal currents, spiralling up on broad wings held rigid in a slight dihedral, upward curved primaries spread like fingers against the sky. It can remain aloft for long periods, moving effortlessly from thermal to thermal with scarcely a movement of the wings. Seen thus, its movements are deceptively slow, and it is easy for the casual observer to underestimate both the speed and agility of which the buzzard is capable—as its impressive, stooping display flights, or the speed with which it can drop out of the sky on to its prey, can testify.

Partly because of its conspicuous aerial behaviour and partly because it is a numerous bird over much of its breeding range, the buzzard lends itself to studies of population density and breeding success and their relationship with habitat and food supply. Many such studies (of varying sophistication) have been carried out on the Continent of Europe (especially in Germany), but few in Britain. The most intensive British study was that of Peter Dare on the edge of Dartmoor during 1956–8. Unfortunately, this remarkably thorough work was never published and remains in the form of a PHD thesis in Exeter University Library. More recently Douglas Weir and Nick Picozzi have been studying the factors affecting population density in Speyside in Inverness-shire, and in the past two decades there have been a number of other useful studies of the population size and reproductive success of buzzards elsewhere in the country. My own study, of the buzzard population of the New Forest in Hampshire, covered the ten years from 1962 until 1971. Its main purposes were to monitor the size and reproductive success of the buzzard population, and to attempt to identify the environmental and other factors controlling these. Much of my interest focused on the territorial behaviour of buzzards as a possible mechanism of population regulation.

This book seeks to describe the history and ecology of the buzzard in Britain. British buzzards belong to the nominate race *Buteo buteo buteo* of a species which breeds across the Palaearctic region from western Europe to Japan. I have leaned heavily on my own experiences in the New Forest, but I have also sought to synthesise the other British work on buzzards and to draw relevant comparisons with continental studies of *B. b. buteo*. If the two chapters on the history of the buzzard in Britain seem to form a disproportionately large part of a mainly biological book it is because the buzzard's history explains much about its present status. The buzzard's history is, moreover, a part of our own social history, and as such is worth the telling.

No book about the buzzard and its history in Britain could be written without incurring a considerable debt to Dr N. W. Moore's key paper on the past and present status of the buzzard in the British Isles (published in *British Birds* in May 1957). I am grateful to Norman Moore and the publishers (H. F. & G. Witherby Ltd) of *British Birds* for allowing me to reproduce two of the figures from this paper and to borrow from two others. I am equally indebted to Dr Peter Dare for permitting me to make use of material from his PHD thesis; to the Royal Society for the Protection of Birds, and especially to Richard Porter, for providing information about the present-day persecution of birds of prey; to the British Trust for Ornithology for allowing me to use ringing recovery data and to reproduce the figures and tables from my analysis of nest record cards for the buzzard (published in *Bird Study* for June 1972); to the late Oliver Hook for letting me utilise his results from small mammal trapping in the New Forest; to Leslie Brown for letting me see and use the draft of the chapter on the buzzard in his forthcoming book on British Birds of Prey; and to R. W. Robson, the Hon Douglas Weir, Shaun White, W. Madge, Pat Gouldsbury (Hon Secretary, Gamekeepers' Association), Professor Donald R. Johnson (University of Idaho), T. A. W. Davis, Leo Batten, Henry Mayer-Gross, and many other friends and correspondents who have at various times so patiently answered my questions about buzzards. The study of the New Forest buzzard populations owed much to the help and enthusiasm over the years of David and Rosemary Billett, Derek Chilcott, Bob Emmett, Len Mummery, Graham Rees, Gerald Westerhoff (whose climbing ability was invaluable), and Eddie Wiseman. I wish to thank the local staff of the Forestry Commission for providing facilities and sometimes equipment for the New Forest buzzard study. I am grateful to Brian Grimes, J. Lawton Roberts, John Marchington, M. J. Helps, A. R. Kitson and the staff of the Zoological Department of the National Museum of Wales for providing the photographs for this book. Finally I wish to acknowledge my debt to my wife, Jennifer, who prepared the manuscript and who has shared with me many hundreds of hours watching buzzards.

C.R.T.

Lyndhurst
Hampshire

Chapter One

THE BUZZARD

The image of the buzzard to emerge repeatedly from older literature is of an indolent and cowardly bird, dependent for a living on whatever small and defenceless creatures it can catch unawares, and much given to idle soaring. 'Unless pressed by hunger it is decidedly sluggish in its habits,' wrote Howard Saunders at the end of the last century.[1] 'He is a sad coward,' commented another nineteenth-century ornithologist, John Wise, 'and the common crow will not only attack, but often defeat him.'[2] Other writers have made similar allusions, all of which are at variance with the evident success that buzzards enjoy where they are not persecuted by that much more ruthless predator, man.

The *Buteo* genus has succeeded in colonising most of the world in one or more of its various forms and species. Buzzards are robust, compact raptors with broad, rather rounded wings and tails. The genus is closely allied to the eagles and, although buzzards are smaller and have relatively smaller, more compressed and less powerful bills, they share the eagle's capacity for using air currents for soaring and for movement over great distances. They appear to have evolved to what might be described as a good compromise design—medium-sized raptors adapted both for seeking prey over large areas by the efficient use of air currents, and for relatively agile movement in confined spaces in the pursuit of prey. Buzzards exploit a great variety of food sources, from earthworms to comparatively large mammals, and it is probable that the genus owes its success to its adaptability and catholicity of taste.

The common buzzard, *Buteo buteo*, is a widespread Palaearctic species, its breeding range extending from the Atlantic islands and the western seaboards of Iberia, France and Britain; across Europe, through Russia and Asia Minor; and in a narrower belt across Siberia to the Sea of Okhostak and Japan. The northern limits of its range approach the 53–62° F July isotherm, which would also appear roughly to coincide with the northern limits of the timber. North of this it is replaced by the rough-legged buzzard *B. lagopus*, with which it also overlaps in Scandinavia. To the south of its range it is replaced by the long-legged buzzard *B. rufinus*, with whose breeding range it overlaps in the near east and the Himalayan region of central Asia. In the Himalayas, a fourth species, *B. hemilasius*, has been distinguished, its range overlapping with both *B. buteo* and *B. rufinus*.

In North America *B. buteo* appears to be replaced ecologically by the red-tailed hawk *B. jamaicensis*, whilst as many as nine other species of *Buteo* (including *B. lagopus*) have been separated on the North American continent. In the Southern Hemisphere, both in the New and Old Worlds, there are, similarly, numerous *Buteo* species, and some authors[3] have considered that forms of *B. buteo* are present in east and south-east Africa and Madagascar, though this view was discarded by the American taxonomist Charles Vaurie.[4]

The populations of *B. buteo* belong to at least three distinct subspecies: *Buteo buteo buteo*, *B. b. vulpinus* and *B. b. japonicus*, and some authors[5] have considered each of these to merit the status of separate species. They do not appear, however, to occupy different ecological niches, which one would expect if this were so, and they replace each other geographically. *B. b. buteo* and *vulpinus* are said to interbreed freely in eastern Europe, where their respective breeding ranges overlap.

The buzzard with which this book is concerned is *B. b. buteo*. This, the typical or nominate race, breeds in Europe north to about 65° in Scandinavia and eastwards to Finland, Rumania and Asia Minor. It is absent from the Shetlands, Faeroes, Iceland and most of Ireland, as well as much of the lowland zone of England. Southwards its range extends to the Mediterranean islands (but not Cyprus) and out into the Atlantic to include the Canaries, Azores and Cape Verde Islands. The buzzards of both the Mediterranean and Atlantic islands have been distinguished as various subspecies by various authors, but it seems doubtful if any of them have a legitimate claim to subspecific status. Certainly Vaurie was unable to find any constant characters to support the recognition of any insular race.[6] To the east, *B. b. buteo* is replaced by and interbreeds with *vulpinus* in a broad zone extending from Fenno-Scandia, south-east through western Russia and the Ukraine, to Rumania. *B. b. vulpinus* breeds from thence eastwards to about longitude 96°; and *japonicus* is the buzzard of eastern Asia and Japan. Some northern populations of all three subspecies migrate south for the winter and many individuals of the *vulpinus* subspecies are then found in western Europe; though the only British record accepted as authentic was of one shot in Wiltshire in September 1864. In Britain *B. b. buteo* is the only representative of the genus to breed and, indeed, the only other *Buteo* to occur at all (apart from the isolated *vulpinus* record) is the rough-legged buzzard, numbers of which appear down the eastern seaboard between October and April.

The plumages of the three *B. buteo* subspecies are variable, and the small differences in measurements and wing formulae, which mainly serve to distinguish them, are too slight to be of much help in the field; though *vulpinus*, which possesses the distinction of an English name, the steppe buzzard, is supposed to be more readily identifiable than most subspecies of raptor. Its wings are somewhat slenderer than those of *buteo*, making the tail appear longer and producing a silhouette somewhat like that of a honey buzzard (which, though not a member of the *Buteo* genus, superficially resembles one).

Buzzards in Britain vary greatly in plumage. Some individuals are almost uniformly dark brown, above and below, in striking contrast to the clear yellow of their feet, legs and cere. At the other extreme, birds occur which are almost completely white on the underside save for dark markings on the underwing coverts. Between these two extremes will be found a multitude of variations, though the most common form is intermediate between them, and is rather lightly barred on the underside with a distinct pectoral band of darker barring. Plumage characters remain constant from year to year—they do not change as the bird moults—and can be of considerable assistance to the observer because they enable him to identify individual birds. Unfortunately, in the area where I know the buzzard best—the New Forest in Hampshire—few noticeably pale or noticeably dark birds occur in the breeding population (though they sometimes turn up during the winter). There may be some significance in the fact that the widest range of plumage variations occurs in areas where the buzzard is most abundant, such as parts of the South-west Peninsula and mid-Wales.

Mainly because of its great variety of plumages, the buzzard can be confused with many other medium-sized raptors, though in flight, and especially when soaring, its silhouette and movements are quite characteristic. In soaring, the wings are noticeably up-tilted, with the angle increasing towards the wingtips, and the primary feathers appearing to curl upwards and inwards. At the same time the wings are pressed forward beyond the head. The tail is fanned in a broad wedge, the outer tail feathers sometimes appearing to touch the trailing edge of the wings. The overall impression, however, is of more importance than details of shape, and this is of a curious rigidity, wings and tail remaining board-like, and moving little in response to air movement even though the bird may be tossed and buffeted in a high wind. In level flight the wing movement is rather stiff, and the wing-beats are shallower than those of most other birds of prey of comparable size. In all its movements the buzzard lacks either the casual fluidity of movement so characteristic of the honey buzzard, with which it is often confused, or the buoyant grace of a kite or harrier. It is chunky, broad-winged, broad-tailed, and short-headed. In Britain, few difficulties of identification should arise. The most authoritative account of the field identification of all the European buzzards will be found in a well-illustrated article by Steen Christensen, Bent Pors Neilson, R. F. Porter and Ian Willis in *British Birds* for June 1971.

Buzzards were described earlier as successful species, and it was suggested that their adaptability to a variety of sources of prey might have largely contributed to this. How successful—how common—is our buzzard in Britain? What ecological niche does it occupy? Ecology involves the assumption that no organism can live in isolation. What then is the buzzard's relationship with its surroundings, with its prey, and with other predators—above all perhaps, with man?

First, what do we know about the numbers of buzzards in Britain? In 1954, Dr N. W. Moore organised national population surveys of the buzzard on behalf of the British Trust for Ornithology, and from the information received he estimated that in 1954 the buzzard population of Britain at the beginning of the breeding season was approximately 12,000 breeding pairs and 2,000 non-breeding birds—a total of 26,000 buzzards. These figures were obtained by direct extrapolation from population data obtained for some 105 census areas covering 6,875 square miles (or about one-fifteenth of the total surface area of the country), and to allow a reasonable margin of error Norman Moore suggested that the total population probably lay between 20,000 and 30,000 birds.[7]

It is arguable that these figures are overestimates. They depend on the 6,875 square miles of census area being a representative sample for the whole of the country. All but a few of the census areas, however, were in good buzzard country in western Britain. Indeed, most census areas were concentrated in districts which have long carried particularly high buzzard populations—central Wales and parts of the South-west Peninsula for example. The eastern counties of England and Scotland, where buzzards are few or absent, were scarcely represented. Nor, indeed, were vast areas of north-west Scotland—for example the blanket bogs of Sutherland—where buzzards have always been thinly or irregularly distributed. Of the 105 census areas only 19 were recorded as having no buzzards—in itself a clear indication of the bias inevitably arising from the difficulty in persuading observers to cover census areas in which they believed there were no buzzards. Moore, of course, recognised this source of bias but felt that it would probably be offset by the tendency of observers in good buzzard country to choose smaller census areas, and by the fact that there were few ornithologists available in many of the areas in which the buzzard was most common, particularly western Scotland. These arguments, however, do not circumvent the fact that all but a very few census areas were in those parts of the country where the buzzard was commonest. The census areas tended to be representative of the northern and western parts of Britain rather than of the country as a whole, and Norman Moore's figures of 20,000–30,000 birds may thus have been an overestimate, conceivably by as much as about 30 per cent.

In 1954 the buzzard population was higher than at any time since the early nineteenth century—the result of a steady build up of numbers following an era of persecution. During and immediately after 1954, the rabbit population, which had formed a major source of food for buzzards, was decimated by myxomatosis. It is probable that many reports of correspondingly drastic decreases in the populations of buzzards were exaggerated, but there is no doubt that the population as a whole slumped, stabilising again at a lower level during the later 1950s; in some districts perhaps not until the end of the decade. In some localities the slump was certainly dramatic, and numbers have not since regained anything approaching their pre-myxomatosis level. Since the myxomatosis episode, further decreases have been reported from some districts of England,[8] though on the other hand the Scottish Highlands and Western Isles population has apparently continued to rise steadily since recovering from the myxomatosis setback. It is very doubtful, however, whether the total British breeding population in 1971 was as high as it was in 1954, and it was probably substantially smaller. On the basis of my own experience of population densities in different parts of western Britain, and on information derived from sources such as County Bird Reports, I would hazard an estimate—more precisely an opinion—of the numbers of buzzards holding territories in the breeding season of 1970 as 8,000–10,000 pairs.

Most of these 8,000–10,000 pairs of buzzards would be in the

South-west Peninsula (the New Forest in Hampshire; Dorset, Somerset, Devon and Cornwall); Wales and the Marches; north-west England (Westmorland, Cumberland, north Lancashire and north-west Yorkshire); Dumfriesshire and Kirkcudbrightshire in the Southern Uplands; and the Scottish Highlands and Western Isles. In Ireland the buzzard maintains little more than a toehold in north-east Ulster. Within these areas of the upland zone of Britain, however, the buzzard is by no means evenly distributed. Moore[9] recorded an average breeding density of one pair per 7·23 square miles for the 1954 buzzard survey census areas, but there was considerable variation from district to district. Densities of over two pairs per square mile were recorded from 5 census areas—Skomer Island, Pembrokeshire; Iona, Argyll; Monmouth; and 2 areas in Devon. On Skomer Island, T. A. W. Davis recorded no less than 8 pairs on 722 acres, a density of 7·08 pairs per square mile.[10] This, however, was quite exceptional, and Moore suggested that 1–2 pairs per square mile was probably the normal maximum in favourable habitat.

What is favourable habitat? Diversity appears to be the key feature. The populations of open moorland, blanket bog, and mountain districts are small—perhaps as much because of the comparative scarcity of nest sites as because of scarcity of food. The breeding pairs tend to be concentrated into valleys radiating outwards from upland massifs, or around the periphery of the hills where farmland and woods increase the variety of both nest sites and prey habitat. For example, in eastern Inverness-shire in 1959 a buzzard population of at least 33 pairs was concentrated into the Spey valley between the Cairngorms and Monadhliaths—a ribbon of mixed farmland, moor, marsh and woodland about seventeen miles long and three and a half miles across, the 1,200ft contour marking the altitude above which buzzards were very seldom known to nest.[11] Like the high moorland and mountain country, the more extensive conifer forests of the uplands support few pairs of buzzards—save around their margins, or where the forest is diversified by intermixed farmland, moor or sheepwalk. It is a fair generalisation that the more uniform the habitat the smaller the buzzard population. Despite its popular image as a bird of the wilderness, the buzzard achieves its densest breeding populations in farmland—admittedly not the intensive arable country of, say, the Wessex chalk or the Midland Plain, but the hilly, mixed farmland of the west, where an abundance of small woods, hedgerows and odd pieces of unreclaimed ground diversify the habitat and provide the greatest variety of prey. The county of Devon, for example, has long supported a large population, save on the open moorlands of Dartmoor and Exmoor. In 1929, H. G. Hurrell calculated that the county carried at least 450 pairs of buzzards.[12] In 1969, Robert Moore thought that the population was not less than 1,000 pairs.[13] The almost innumerable well wooded valleys threading through a landscape of well hedged mixed farmland with many small pieces of rough ground would seem to be the optimum habitat for buzzards.

Although sparse over large tracts of mountain, blanket bog, moorland and forest, the buzzard is undoubtedly the most numerous raptor within much of its breeding range in Britain. This breeding range is shared with ten other common species of vertebrate predator, apart from man. These are the sparrowhawk, kestrel, tawny owl, fox, stoat, weasel, badger (perhaps better described as an omnivore), adder, grass snake (which is, however, absent from Scotland), and domestic cat. In Wales and the Marches, and in south-west England—it does not occur further north—the little owl could be added. In the Scottish Highlands and Western Isles the golden eagle, with a population which may be as high as 300 pairs[14] could justifiably be included in the list. Locally, other species could also be added—for example, the hen harrier in the Outer Hebrides, Orkneys and many districts of the Highlands; and the red kite in some parts of Wales.

To what extent is there competition between these species? According to Gause's principle,[15] the feeding niches of the different predators are never precisely similar, though they may often overlap: the majority of the predators mentioned are, for example, dependent in varying degrees on small mammal populations, especially short-tailed voles. Some predators, like the kestrel and sparrowhawk, are relatively highly specialised, not only in their normal prey but in their manner of obtaining it—in the one case by detecting the quarry (mainly small rodents, and in most districts especially short-tailed voles) whilst hovering, and securing it after a vertical dive, and in the other by snatching the quarry (small and medium-sized birds) in horizontal flight, using a combination of speed and surprise. Other species, like the golden eagle, buzzard and red kite, are much more generalised feeders and tend to be more versatile in their methods of obtaining prey, though the soaring habit is common to all three species as a means of locating prey over large areas with the minimum of effort.

In reality the overlap in the prey spectra of the different predators is often smaller than at first appears because different predators preying on the same prey species tend to hunt in different habitats, or at different times of the day, or prey on different components of the population of the prey species.[16] Kestrels and tawny owls both feed extensively on short-tailed voles, but the former species hunts by day and in open habitats, and the latter by night and in woodland. Buzzards and golden eagles both take carrion, but in the Highlands buzzards tend to be confined to the valleys and lower ground, and the eagles to range over the higher moors and mountains. Both stoats and weasels prey regularly on rabbits, but stoats tend to kill heavier animals than weasels. This is not to say that instances of direct competition for food do not occur between predators. Buzzards and red kites (and also ravens) sometimes squabble over sheep carrion. Occasional incidents have been reported in which a kestrel and a weasel have met in pursuit of the same vole. As a general rule, however, competition between predators for prey is likely to be intraspecific rather than interspecific because their prey niches are different.

The buzzard draws on a wide range of food sources. The prey of a pair of buzzards during the breeding season is likely to include a bewildering variety of items, but the most frequent prey in most localities in Britain today will undoubtedly be small mammals—mainly short-tailed voles, but also shrews, moles, bank voles, and wood mice. The rabbit still qualifies as a major prey species, and before myxomatosis, of course, it was probably the most important single source of food for the buzzard over much of Britain. Other important food sources include birds (mainly passerines ranging in size from blackbird to woodpigeon); reptiles (adders, grass snakes, slow-worms and common lizards); amphibians (mainly common frogs); beetles and other insects; and earthworms. Carrion (and the placenta of ewes) is taken where it is available, and in parts of the uplands it qualifies as an important part of the diet. Other more locally exploited prey are the chicks of wading birds such as redshank and curlew; the young of gamebirds; hares (mainly leverets); and brown rats, usually caught around ricks. Other prey recorded from time to time includes such unlikely items as fish (usually trout on the rare occasions they are identified), weasels, stoats, kestrels, and young tawny owls.

Seabird colonies are often exploited by coastal breeding buzzards. On Skomer Island, off the Pembrokeshire coast, for example, puffins as well as rabbits were recorded by Davis and Saunders[17] as the staple diet of fledgling buzzards during the period 1954–64. Rabbits were thought to be the main food outside the breeding season, though an analysis of 68 pellets collected on the island in autumn 1960 mainly yielded the remains of small mammals (voles, wood mice and shrews) and small birds, together with a lizard, three frogs, beetles and earthworms.

In the New Forest, in Hampshire, birds form a large proportion of the prey during the breeding season, and probably at other times, and a remarkably wide range of species have been recorded from nests. Here the concentration on avian prey may well arise more from a relative deficiency in small mammals than from a particular abundance or availability of birds.[18] New Forest buzzards also take grey squirrels, and no doubt both this species and the red squirrel are taken regularly elsewhere.

In the Postbridge area on the edge of Dartmoor, the buzzard population studied by Peter Dare during 1956–8[19] immediately after myxomatosis, depended heavily on voles and other small mammals, though they continued to hunt the residual rabbit population and, as Dare remarked, were far more effective in winkling out the survivors of myxomatosis than were the Ministry of Agriculture. Analysis of regurgitated pellets yielded the remains of 774 mammals, of which 193 were rabbits and 364 were voles; 103 birds (but no game or poultry); 55 reptiles, of which 29 were adders; and 131 amphibia, of which 121 were frogs. In addition there were abundant invertebrate remains, mainly of beetles and lepidoptera larvae. Dare also identified a total of 508 prey items brought to buzzards' nests—345 mammals, of which 120 were rabbits and 134 were voles; 73 birds; 15 reptiles (13 adders); and 60 amphibia, mainly frogs.

Avian prey was taken mainly when the buzzards had chicks to feed. Among the species recorded were adult starlings, blackbirds, song thrushes, woodpigeons, magpies and carrion crows, and fledgling carrion crows and small passerines such as meadow pipits and skylarks. Lizards and snakes clearly formed an important supplementary food source during the spring and summer, whilst frogs were hunted mainly in the early spring before their post-spawning dispersal. Dare emphasised the extent to which invertebrate prey—dung beetles, ground beetles, caterpillars, leather-jackets and earthworms—were taken, though by weight they clearly comprised only a small proportion of the buzzards' diet.

That rabbits are still taken in substantial numbers where they are available is illustrated by the list of prey recorded by L. MacNally for a buzzard's nest with young, near Fort Augustus, Inverness-shire, in 1962.[20] On 43 visits on consecutive days he found a total of 32 rabbits, 19 moles, 5 frogs, 4 voles, 8 birds (a snipe, a black-headed gull, a young cuckoo, 2 fledgling song thrushes, 2 fledgling robins, and a fledgling dipper), and 5 pieces of lamb carrion thought to have been taken from the entrance to a fox's earth on the opposite side of the valley. That few voles were recorded was probably because they are usually eaten at once by young buzzards—a fact which has always to be remembered when analysing prey remains from buzzards' nests. The comparatively large number of moles found on the nest is interesting. In the nineteenth and early twentieth centuries, many writers alluded to the buzzard's supposed preference for moles. 'As to the food of the Common Buzzard,' wrote J. E. Harting in 1901, 'W. T. Andrews, taxidermist of Swansea, having examined many specimens at all seasons of the year, states that he has never found any feathers in the crop but invariably the partly digested remains of the common mole.'[21] In 1903, F. O. Morris observed that the buzzard 'destroys numberless moles, of which it seems particularly fond,' and adds that buzzards caught them 'by watching patiently by their haunts, until the moving of the earth . . . points out to him their exact locality.'[22] One might be tempted to observe that mole-catching buzzards were just the sort of natural phenomenon that Victorians or Edwardians might be expected to perpetuate and embellish, but in Wales in 1965 I watched a buzzard catch a mole in more or less the manner described by Morris. The buzzard had been standing in a small meadow for some time, perfectly still apart from movements of the head. Quite suddenly it ran rapidly across the short, sheep-bitten turf to pounce on what later transpired to be a mole-run immediately below the surface—presumably the bird had seen some movement of soil as the mole worked its way along the run. The incident occurred so rapidly that it was difficult to absorb the details of the kill, but after a brief assault at the earth with its talons the buzzard could be seen standing on a glossy black object. It remained thus for several minutes, looking about it and, more occasionally, looking down at its prey. Finally it took wing, the mole dangling from its outstretched talons as it gained height.

There is no doubt that moles are caught regularly by buzzards, and many at least must be caught in this fashion. Moles do, however, move about on the surface more than is generally appreciated, particularly the young during their dispersal in late June and July. Moles have been recorded in most of the systematic studies of the prey brought to buzzards' nests at this time. Indeed, in Poland in 1953, Zygamunt Czarnecki and Tadeusz Foksowicz found that of 367 vertebrates brought by the adults to two nests under observation during the fledgling period, the majority were moles, the common vole forming only the second most important prey.[23] Moles were in this case reported to be exceptionally numerous in the locality, and numbers were found dead on the surface by the observers, suggesting that some may have been picked up as carrion by the buzzards.

The buzzard's diet has been widely studied in central and northern Europe, and the literature on the subject is extensive. The variety of organisms taken is as wide as in Britain, but most accounts agree that small mammals, mostly common voles, usually form around 50 per cent of the prey recorded as being taken during the breeding season,[24] whilst at a nest studied by Jan Pinowski and Lech Ryszkowski in western Pomorze, Poland, in 1959, common voles formed as much as 80 per cent of the prey brought to a nest containing a single young bird.[25] In a more recent study of the ecology of birds of prey in Lorraine, in north-east France, Jean-Marc Thiollay found that small mammals, mainly common voles, bank voles and wood mice, formed about 40 per cent of the vertebrate prey identified, summer and winter. Of 4,042 items of vertebrate prey recorded, 1,963 were small mammals; 977 were medium sized mammals, mainly (833) moles; 44 were large mammals (including less than a dozen rabbits); 814 were birds, mainly small- and medium-sized passerines; 46 were—interestingly—fish, apparently found in lakes as they dried out in the autumn; and 198 were frogs and reptiles. Invertebrate prey—mostly beetles and grubs—was also taken in large quantities, and Thiollay considered that individual buzzards sometimes depended heavily on this source of food. His data was collected over the period October 1965 to July 1966, and in his analysis he distinguished between the October–March and April–July periods, which showed that the numbers of birds and moles in the diet increased markedly during the breeding season, presumably in response to the need to find larger prey items to feed growing broods. Thiollay, like other workers, was clearly impressed with the opportunism exhibited by the buzzard in exploiting a wide variety of prey sources as they became available.[26]

The insignificant number of rabbits in the diet of the Lorraine buzzards appears to be typical of the continental buzzard populations which have been studied. The distribution of the rabbit on the continent includes the Iberian Peninsula, France, Belgium, Holland, Germany and much of central Europe; but the rabbit, for reasons which are far from clear, appears never to have become an important prey species of the buzzard outside Britain. That the buzzard has always been popularly associated with small mammals on the continent is confirmed by the German vernacular *Mäusebussard* and Danish *Musvaagen*. The common vole is of sufficient importance on the continent for the number of eggs laid and young reared by buzzards in many areas to vary significantly according to their abundance.

It will be evident that a major ecological characteristic of the buzzard is its capacity for spanning a wide range of food sources within limits of prey size and weight, marked at one extreme by insect larvae and at the other by half-grown rabbits. Within these limits there is a tendency to concentrate on mammalian prey in more or less open habitats; but the buzzard possesses a capacity for adapting its hunting behaviour to exploit whatever other prey is readily available. Most prey, perhaps, is caught after being sighted by a hovering or circling bird two or three hundred feet above it. The buzzard drops a little on partly-closed wings, pauses, drops again and then, slowly at first, then gathering speed in a final, often almost vertical rush on closing wings, it makes its stoop. On three occasions out of four, the bird pulls out well above the ground. The prey has moved. On the fourth occasion the bird's wings open again as the ground rushes to meet it and the outstretched yellow talons drive home into the prey. Not all successful stoops are spectacular. Often the final approach is a gentle glide, the final short rush terminating with a flurry of wings as the bird checks and twists down on to the prey—perhaps in this case a frog or some other comparatively slow-moving animal. For so comparatively clumsy-looking a bird the buzzard is adept at hovering, the body remaining quite still whilst the flickering wings maintain its position, head to wind. Hovering, however, tends to be employed over large tracts of open country where there are few or no perches. Where there are trees or poles it will use those, and from such observation posts the bird is probably able to find prey by ear as well as by eye. The head is often cocked this way and that—exactly as though the bird were listening for the squeal of a vole in the grass beneath it. Once the prey is located exactly, the bird leaves its perch and descends in a deceptively slow glide, only the final second before the kill giving any impression of the deadliness of its purpose.

Besides hunting from posts or trees, or by observing the ground from aloft, the buzzard is surprisingly competent at hunting birds through tree tops or among low cover in the manner of a sparrow-hawk. It can also display remarkable agility in pursuit of a squirrel around the stem of a tree, though I have to admit that on not one of the four occasions (all in the New Forest) on which I have witnessed this was the squirrel actually caught. On the ground, too, the buzzard is more agile than might be anticipated. It can run very rapidly, and I have already mentioned its ability to catch moles as they break the surface of the soil. I have also many records (almost all from Wales) of buzzards behaving in an almost thrush-like manner in search of earthworms and insects—a short, rapid run, a pause, and then a sudden dart at a worm or perhaps a beetle. I have watched worms dealt with in precisely the way Harting described seventy years ago. The bird would 'draw it out of the soil, bite it in several pieces about an inch in length and swallow them separately'.[27] Regular ground-feeding by buzzards during autumn 1968 near Sidmouth, in Devon, has been described by R. W. Hayman, and it is worth quoting from his account.

> A field of about seven acres had been newly sown with grass in early August; by mid-September the new grass was appearing thinly, and from that time on this field proved attractive to buzzards. On the 21st there were three, and by the 27th the pattern of behaviour had apparently stabilised with four or five buzzards well spaced out over the field for most of the day. The number seldom fell below two, except when mist and rain kept them away completely, and the maximum was seven on 4th and 7th October. Their feeding behaviour consisted of standing still, looking around and then clumsily walking or running a short distance to pick up in the bill small items of food which were immediately swallowed. None of this food could be identified, but frequent defecations suggested ample supplies. The earliest buzzards would usually arrive well before sunrise, often

> calling as they came overhead, and they frequently continued feeding until dusk before making off for the night . . . By 18th November the field had apparently lost much of its attraction . . . possibly because of the thickening of the grass cover or some seasonal reduction in the food supply, and subsequently it seldom held more than one buzzard.[28]

Pinowski and Ryszkowski[29] give an interesting account of the manner in which buzzards in their study area modified their hunting in winter according to the availability of food. The study area comprised a coypu farm which was 474 acres of reed, sedge, canals and a lake; and a surrounding area of woods and fields. In winter the coypu were caught and confined in large pens where they were fed with oats. In the breeding season the three pairs of buzzards in the study area hunted mainly over the fields, where their main prey was common voles. In the winter

> . . . the buzzards modified their hunting according to the availability of food, which, in turn was dependent on the weather. Early in the winter they still hunted more in the adjacent fields where the vegetation was short than on the farm where it was high, but they quickly exploited a temporary source of food when the farm was flooded and islands of higher ground were crowded with small mammals. Again, when there was deep snow they preyed almost exclusively on the small birds which gathered at the coypu pens. In attacking the flocks of yellowhammers there, they depended on surprise and appeared suddenly from behind stacks of straw after watching from an adjacent fence.

The coypu themselves were evidently rather too much for a buzzard to cope with normally, and only one instance of a kill was recorded, though coypu carrion was taken more frequently.

Because of its versatility as a predator, and its capacity for spanning a wide range of food sources, the buzzard is unlikely to be adversely affected by competition with other predators for food. These characteristics also enable the species to achieve high densities of population. This does not mean that competition with other species does not occur. Buzzards, ravens and red kites, for example, certainly compete for sheep carrion in Wales, and I have heard a number of accounts in which the three species met at the same carcase, though I have never witnessed such an event myself. In most of these incidents, however, the buzzard was successful in maintaining the dominant position whilst it gorged itself. Ravens, especially when working in pairs, were successful in filching food from the buzzard and moved on to the carcase when the buzzard had fed. Red kites tended to be last in the pecking order and, as the kite depends heavily on carrion in Wales, it is not inconceivable that competition with buzzards and ravens is now a factor limiting its population there.

Whilst competition with other species for food is unlikely to be a significant factor in limiting buzzard populations, competition with ravens for nest sites in open moorland and hill country, where nesting crags are relatively few, may be important. Ravens start breeding much earlier than buzzards—often in February—and the presence of a buzzard anywhere near their nests invariably provokes them to aggression. It is true that the buzzard generally evades the raven's repeated headlong rushes with effortless side-slips (occasionally presenting its talons if the attack presses too close), and often one cannot but feel that the aerial battles are prompted mostly by exuberance: but, nevertheless, it is usually the buzzard which breaks away from the engagement by leaving in a fast glide or, when it can, by soaring higher, and it is likely that constant harassment prevents many potential buzzard nest sites near occupied ravens' nests from being used. Aerial encounters between buzzards and peregrines (another early nester) are also frequent, and it is rare for buzzards to nest near an occupied peregrine eyrie, though they may actually use one if the peregrines are absent.

To what extent is predation by the buzzard likely to affect the populations of its prey; and, conversely, to what extent are fluctuations in prey populations likely to affect the buzzard?

It is natural to assume that predators must function as regulators of the numbers of their prey. It is often argued, however, that predators in general merely cull the prey populations of a surplus which would in any case perish because of limitations imposed on the population by food supply and other environmental factors, and as a generalisation this is almost certainly true. It is, moreover, true that (again as a generalisation) predators tend to cull the weak and sickly from the prey population. On the other hand, I believe there may be instances in which predators hold down prey populations below environmental capacity. Sparrowhawks, for example, concentrate on small to medium-sized woodland birds, and hunt within comparatively small territories. Where undisturbed by human predation they achieve high density populations. I believe they may well have a strongly depressant effect on the populations of many of the birds upon which they feed. Similarly, it is possible that buzzards exert a definite control on the size of residual rabbit populations in some areas. The contribution of predation to the regulation of prey populations, however, becomes proportionately smaller if the reproductive capacity of the prey species increases rapidly in proportion to that of the predators. This happens periodically with some small mammals, especially voles, and indeed happened on a longer time scale when the rabbit population 'exploded' in the nineteenth century. On these occasions the prey population 'escapes' above a level below which it is vulnerable to predator control. Predators alone have never succeeded in bringing the periodic build-ups in vole populations back to 'normal' again. It took a disease, not predation, to bring about the population 'crash' in the rabbit.[30]

As a species, the buzzard tends to feed on whatever prey under a certain size limit is readily available and most easily caught, though individual birds may concentrate on particular prey species and ignore others which appear to the human observer to offer an easier living. Because of its catholicity of taste, it is unlikely that the buzzard alone very often removes a significant proportion of the population of any one of its prey species. I have suggested that buzzards may hold down residual rabbit populations, and there may be other examples of a positive relationship with prey species, in addition to which the buzzard may contribute to the regulation of some prey species—one immediately thinks of small mammals—by the collective predator force which they support.

If predation does not often affect the population of any one prey species, it is not true, conversely, that fluctuations in prey populations always leave predator populations unaffected. In particular, both the breeding populations and the output of young of some raptors vary with the cyclic fluctuations common in the populations of the small mammals on which they mainly feed. D. W. Snow, for example, showed that the years in which the largest numbers of nestling kestrels were ringed in northern England and southern Scotland coincided with a particular abundance of the species' main prey there, the short-tailed vole.[31] H. N. Southern, in his classic study of the tawny owl population of Wytham Woods, near Oxford, between 1947 and 1959, showed that there was a direct relationship between the breeding success of the owls and the numbers of the wood mice and bank voles on which they mainly fed. In 1958, when the mouse and vole populations were particularly low, no owls even attempted to breed.[32]

Because it is a generalised feeder, the buzzard tends to be insulated against fluctuations in breeding success and numbers arising from a variable prey-biomass. Nevertheless, there was a definite reaction in the buzzard population when the rabbit population was decimated by myxomatosis in the 1950s. As was remarked earlier in this chapter, many reports of breeding failure and population declines were probably exaggerated, but the species was undoubtedly adversely affected by the decline in the rabbit population. The rabbit was so abundant and so readily caught that in many districts it formed a disproportionately large part of the total prey-biomass. Because of the high rabbit population, the buzzard was able to maintain exceptionally high density populations. The virtual removal of the rabbit could clearly only result in a reduction in the numbers of buzzards—that is, adaption to a lower prey-biomass. In most districts this seems to have occurred within two or three years after an initial period when interspecific competition resulted in widespread breeding failure. There is some evidence that since myxomatosis the buzzards in some sheepwalk areas of northern Britain have become increasingly dependent on short-tailed voles, and that their breeding success now fluctuates in a way similar to that of kestrels.[33] There would seem to be a difference in the response of the two raptors, however, in that during good vole years the actual number of pairs of kestrels breeding increases, though the brood size does not, whereas the buzzards show a slight increase in the numbers of young reared, the number of breeding pairs remaining the same.

In sum, the buzzard is an unspecialised and versatile predator, relatively well insulated against catastrophe from declines in the numbers of any part of its prey spectrum. It is capable of breeding at comparatively high densities where prey and nest sites are abundant, and is, moreover, able to adapt to a considerable variety of country. It is thus potentially a successful species—the more so since it can achieve a fairly high rate of reproduction and is reasonably long-lived. As Norman Moore remarked, it is well adapted to a world in which habitats change rapidly. It would undoubtedly be more numerous and more widespread in Britain today but for the activities of man.

Man has affected the numbers and distribution of buzzards both by direct predation and, indirectly, by interfering with the food chain of which it is part, though in the latter instance the buzzard has been insulated against catastrophe by its versatility. The introduction of the virus *Myxomatosis cuniculus* into the rabbit population, and the secondary effects on the buzzard population, have already been referred to. The use of toxic chemicals in agriculture is another recent manifestation of man's capacity for meddling with the food chain. The effects of toxic insecticides on populations of birds of prey in the 1950s and 1960s is now well documented.[34] Briefly, it has been shown that organochlorine pesticides have found their way into predator populations, via the prey, after having been used as seed dressings or in sheep-dips. The organochlorines are cumulative, and the occurrence of comparatively high residues in species such as the peregrine, golden eagle, and sparrowhawk (and their eggs) has been clearly associated with widespread breeding failure, egg-breaking by the adult birds, and decreasing populations. Decreasing eggshell thickness has been an associated (and in itself partly causal) phenomenon.[35]

The buzzard has been one of the predatory birds least affected—probably because of its catholicity of diet. The ways by which insecticide residues have reached predatory birds have been mainly through birds which have picked up residues from arable land, and from sheep carrion which had been contaminated by the use of organochlorines in sheep-dips. The buzzard draws on both sources of food, but in most areas depends extensively on neither. In consequence, the buzzard population as a whole appears to have become only minimally contaminated, though it would be unwise to dismiss some local declines in numbers during the late 1950s and early 1960s as being unassociated with toxic chemicals.

The buzzard's ecological characteristics are no protection against the gun and pole-trap, and man the predator has had a profound effect on buzzard numbers and distribution. Three centuries ago the buzzard was a familiar bird throughout Britain. Today it is mainly a species of the north and west, and it has become so because of man's persecution, arising from his belief that the buzzard competed with him for food and reduced the numbers of game-birds he could rear for sport. The era of intensive persecution was brought to an end by the departure of the gamekeeper for another war of attrition between 1914 and 1918. Between the wars there was something of a revival of persecution, and this has happened again in more recent years. Theoretically the buzzard is protected by law, but it is probable that persecution by man still places a major constraint on buzzard numbers and distribution in Britain.

Chapter Two

DECLINE

c1600–1914

Man's persecution of other vertebrate predators is part of the story of his struggle for dominance over his environment, and probably commenced four or five thousand years ago with the innovation of domesticated animals during the Neolithic period. Carnivorous mammals and birds preyed on man's stock and thus competed directly with him for protein. It is unlikely, however, that man brought about more than local extinctions of other predators in Europe much before the end of the first millennium AD. By that time a significant proportion of the land surface of the continent—including Britain—had been cleared of its early woodland cover, and a more or less permanent pattern of human settlement was emerging. As the settled area expanded and the woodland retracted so the larger, more conspicuous and most challenging of man's competitors were urged down the road to extinction. In Britain the brown bear had probably become extinct by the tenth century.[1] The wolf was systematically persecuted through the Middle Ages, and it is a matter for surprise that it persisted as late as the end of the fifteenth century in even remote parts of England, and until much later still in Scotland and Ireland. The last wolf was killed in Scotland in 1743. In Ireland there were still wolf packs early in the eighteenth century, and the last survivor was not killed until 1770.[2]

Written evidence is scanty, but the smaller predators—for example, the polecat and pine marten, and birds like the buzzard and sparrowhawk—appear to have received little systematic persecution before the second half of the sixteenth century. Indeed, some birds of prey—particularly the peregrine—were carefully protected for falconry, whilst both red kites and ravens were protected as essential domestic scavengers in medieval and sixteenth-century London, where refuse disposal arrangements were otherwise rudimentary. Owls, too, were often protected—or at least spared persecution—because they were regarded as useful predators of some of the small rodents to whom man played a reluctant host. Most predators, however, the buzzard among them, had clearly long been regarded as pests—takers of lambs and domestic fowl—and in fact as early as 1457 an Act of James II of Scotland listed many—including the buzzard—as vermin to be destroyed. During the sixteenth century in England there was a succession of enactments which, among other things, encouraged the destruction of vermin, mainly by making obligatory the payment by churchwardens of rewards financed from local levies on land or tithes. Churchwardens' disbursement or account books from the late sixteenth century through into the nineteenth contain much information of importance in elucidating the faunal history of England during that period, though for various reasons they have to be interpreted with caution.

Churchwardens' accounts are the main source of information about the buzzard in Britain before the beginning of the nineteenth century, though the species is mentioned, mostly in fairly general terms, by a number of the early ornithological writers. William Turner—the father of British ornithology, as James Fisher and others called him—mentioned the bird in *Avium Praecipuarum*, the first printed work about birds, in 1544, and he clearly regarded it as common then.[3] Francis Willughby described the buzzard in his *Ornithologia*, which was published in 1676 and translated into English two years later by his friend John Ray; and though he did not refer specifically to its status, the unwritten assumption is that it remained common at that time. He gives a remarkably accurate picture of its prey, which serves to emphasise that even in the seventeenth century some would have acquitted the buzzard of preying on the farmyard, though perhaps not on the warren.

It feeds [he writes] not only upon Mice and Moles but also upon birds:

> for out of the stomach of one that we opened we took a small bird entire, and out of the stomach of another even a thrush. It is a great destroyer of *Conies*: yet for want of better food it will feed on Beetles, Earth-Worms and other insects.[4]

A hundred years later, Thomas Pennant described the buzzard as 'the commonest of the hawk kind we have in England',[5] and in 1781 John Latham remarked that it was a bird 'known by everyone'.[6] In view of the persecution recorded in churchwardens' accounts, these generalisations may be a less than accurate picture of the buzzard's situation at the end of the eighteenth century, and this is supported by some of the nineteenth-century writers. For the nineteenth century there is an almost embarrassing wealth of contemporary writing which collectively documents the buzzard's continued persecution and the decline of the species to an all-time low at the end of the century. The long period of ill-fortune, from the sixteenth century to the beginning of the present one, forms the subject of this chapter. The species' more recent history is traced in Chapter Three.

The Tudor vermin legislation was aimed mainly at grain-eating birds and reflects government concern for arable production at a time of rising population, a concern sharpened by the contraction of the arable acreage which had taken place through the widespread enclosure of open fields and their subsequent conversion to sheep pasture.[7] The first enactment, in 1532 (24 Hen VIII, c 10) provided that because of the 'inumerable number' of 'rooks, crows and choughs', every parish, township and hamlet should provide itself with nets for their destruction, and that two pence was to be paid by the owner of the land or manor for every dozen crows, rooks or choughs killed. In 1566 'An Acte for the preservacion of Grayne' (8 Eliz I, c 15) approached vermin control in a more comprehensively ruthless spirit, extending its scope beyond the confirmed grain-eaters to include most birds and mammals which could conceivably compete with man. The provisions of the earlier Act of 1532 were reiterated, and it was further enacted that the churchwardens, with six parishioners, should levy a rate on the holders of lands or tithes to provide a fund from which they should pay rewards for the destruction of 'noyfull Fowles and Vermyn'. Payment was usually made on the production of the victims' heads:

> old Crowes, Choughs, Pyes, or Rookes, for the heades of every three of them one penny and for the heades of every six young Crowes, Choughs, Pyes or Rookes, one penny; and for every six egges of any of them unbroken one penny; and like wise for every twelve Stares [starling] Heades a penny: For everie Head of Martyn, Hawkes [ie sparrowhawk], Furskytte [stoat], Moldekytte [weasel], Busarde, Shagge, Cormerat, or Ryngtale [harrier], two pence; and for every two Egges of them one penney; and for every Iron [heron] or Osprayes Heade Fower Pence; for the Head of every Woodwall [woodpecker], Pye, Jaye, Raven, or Kyte, one penney; for the Heade of everie Byrde which is called the Kinges Fysshr [probably the dipper not the kingfisher], one penney; for the Heade of everie Bulfynche or other Byrde that devoureth the blowth of Fruite, one penney; for the Heades of everie Fox or Gray [badger] twelve pence; and for the Heades of every three Rattes or twelve Myse, one penney; for the Heades of everie Moldewarpe or Wante [mole] one halfpenney.

The Act of 1566 was strengthened and enlarged by further enactments of 1572 (14 Eliz I, c 11) and 1598 (39 Eliz I, c 18) which, among other things, extended the vermin list and provided penalties for failure to control vermin. J. C. Cox showed that the vermin acts were widely implemented during the sixteenth and seventeenth centuries,[8] though their precise interpretation seems to have varied from parish to parish and decade to decade depending, apparently, on the relative local abundance of the different pest species, the amount of money available for payments, and the opinions of the churchwardens as to which particular species were the most noxious and whose destruction should therefore be most encouraged. Some churchwardens seem to have confined payments to grain-eating birds—rooks ('crows' in most accounts)—or to such notorious trespassers in the farmyard as badgers and foxes and the odd buzzard or kite. Others were evidently willing to pay for virtually any head brought to them. Cox cites the example of

Bishops Stortford, in Hertfordshire, where between April 1569 and April 1571 Edward Wagley received £2 12s 7½d for 141 hedgehogs, 53 moles, 6 weasels, 1 polecat, 1,476 mice, 80 rats, 202 crows' eggs and 154 crows' heads, 128 magpies' eggs, 24 starlings' heads, 5 hawks' heads and 5 kingfishers' heads. Parallels will be found in most parish histories. The amount and variety of wildlife destroyed was often prodigious, and even birds such as tits—'urchins'—were sometimes pronounced vermin. In some parishes certain individuals seem to have become professional (or at least regular) vermin catchers, either self-appointed or by agreement with the churchwardens—witness, for example, payments in the 1690s to the 'roant-catcher' of Ovington in Hampshire.[9]

Because of the variety of local circumstances under which vermin payments were made, and because few series of accounts have been systematically analysed, it is difficult to draw general conclusions about the intensity with which different species were persecuted at different times and in different regions. It would be fair to suggest, however, that grain-eating birds (especially rooks) and rodents, and the predatory mammals, bore the brunt of the initial assault in the sixteenth and early seventeenth centuries. L. Mascell, in a work ominously entitled *Sundrie Engines and Trappes*, published in 1590, gives illustrations of a variety of traps for catching them. Records of payments for the heads of birds of prey—usually 'hawks', kites or buzzards—are frequent, but not sufficiently so to suggest any concerted campaign against them. The churchwardens' accounts for Minchinhampton, in Gloucestershire, for example, mention payments for buzzards in 1575, but then not again until 1596 and again, after an even longer gap, in 1634.[10] Around the middle of the seventeenth century there seems to have been something of a lull in the vermin campaign. But then, after the Restoration, the assault began again in earnest and this time it concentrated not only upon the grain-eaters but also upon buzzards, kites and ravens—predators, it would be alleged, of lambs and farmyard poultry, not to mention rabbits which were a valued food source maintained for the most part, more or less artificially in open warrens.[11] From about 1670 there are abundant references to payments for all three species in churchwardens' accounts from Cornwall to Lincolnshire.

In interpreting the payments for kites and buzzards it is well to question the extent to which the two species were confused. Besides their modern vernacular names, the buzzard was also known as the puttock, and the kite as the glede. However, this seems only to have been a very general rule, and the four names were to some extent interchangeable; though the term kite seems most often to have been used to mean any larger raptor, whilst glede meant a kite, and puttock a buzzard. In 1891, Borrer remarked that in Sussex during his youth, buzzards, if distinguished at all, were called puttocks, but that usually all large hawks went indiscriminately by the name of kite.[12] In Devon the buzzard was commonly called the kitt or keat.[13] In Cumberland it had the more distinctive though unattractive appellation of shreak.[14] In churchwardens' accounts, kites occur more often than buzzards and often to the complete exclusion of buzzards. The subject could stand better researching but I feel confident that—as in the field so in the vestry—the churchwarden, when confronted with the victims' heads, tended to enter them all as kites rather than distinguish them specifically. Doubtless it was for this reason that kites and buzzards came to have a similar price on their heads; though in the Act of 1566 the payment for a kite was to be one penny and that for a buzzard two pence.

Perhaps the most illuminating series of accounts—because of their wealth of detail—are those of the churchwardens of Tenterden in the Weald of Kent, analysed by N. F. Ticehurst half a century ago.[15] They run from 1626 to 1712 and show that the major vermin drive began in 1676. Prior to that date the entries refer mainly to foxes, polecats, hedgehogs, crows and magpies. Only 3 buzzards—a brood of 3 young taken in 1629—and 14 ravens, were mentioned before 1675. The first kite was recorded in 1654 and from then until 1675 no more than 3 were paid for in any one year. In 1676, however, there commenced what Ticehurst described as 'an intensive campaign for the thinning-out of vermin', which this time included the avian predators. It lasted about fourteen years, during which time payments were made for 56 buzzards and 198 ravens. No less than 380 kites were paid for between 1676 and 1686, numbers dropping away thereafter to annual totals of 35, 13, 2 and 2. Many of the buzzards and kites were clearly taken as young birds in the nest. After 1690 the pressure seems to have slackened—indeed, the price seems temporarily to have been removed from the heads of crows, rooks, jackdaws and magpies, though it was put on again in 1697. After that date a further drastic thinning-out of vermin seems to have commenced, though unfortunately no details other than the total sums expended each year are then given in the accounts.

The campaign at Tenterden had its counterparts elsewhere—though I have seen no other reference to so large a number of predators being killed in so short a space of time—but it cannot be assumed that it reflected a completely universal trend. Certainly it seems to have mirrored events in much of lowland Britain—especially perhaps in the midland counties—but there were clearly extensive areas where birds of prey went without a price on their heads. This seems to have been generally true of the Wessex chalk. Hampshire churchwardens' accounts, for example, record fairly regular payments for polecats, foxes, hedgehogs, badgers and house sparrows, from about 1670—though few payments for any vermin before that date—but I have been unable to find a single reference to a bird of prey.[16] Probably the raptor populations on the bare chalklands were too small to justify subsidised destruction.

The vermin campaign was by no means confined to the lowland zone. There are indications that in many parts of upland Britain in the late seventeenth and in the eighteenth centuries the churchwardens often supported a campaign against birds and mammals considered to be predators of farm and farmyard stock. At Sidbury, in Devon, for example, where there was a large and varied vermin kill from 1622 onwards, raptors—mainly kites—appear first in 1677 and are thereafter frequent. At St Neots in Cornwall, most of the fifty kites mentioned between 1621 and 1700 were paid for after 1675. At Crosby in Lancashire, kites and 'hawks' were killed systematically in the first three decades of the eighteenth century.

In the Lake District, golden eagles were an additional subject of persecution, and in the early eighteenth century the substantial sum of 12d was being paid for adult birds. At Borrowdale, eagles' eyries were raided annually, and a special rope was kept in the valley for the purpose.[17]

In so far as it is reflected in the account books of churchwardens, the campaign against predatory birds, and indeed many other alleged pests, drew to a close towards the middle of the eighteenth century. Increasingly from the 1720s, and in many parishes almost exclusively after the 1750s and 1760s, the churchwardens concentrated their support on the control of house sparrows, a bird whose population undoubtedly underwent an explosive increase after the seventeenth century (associated with the expansion of enclosure and cultivation). Indeed, in many Hampshire parishes, sparrows had been slaughtered in large numbers since the 1670s: at Rockbourne, payments were made for as many as seventy-two dozen heads in 1687 alone,[18] and this was no isolated instance. In some counties literally millions of sparrows were killed in the eighteenth and early nineteenth centuries.[19] In the nineteenth century the rook —whose population also increased with the expansion of farmland habitats—joined the sparrow as a target for organised persecution.

What explanation can be offered for the initiation of the campaign against predators in the immediate post-Restoration period, and its cessation some seventy or eighty years later?

The post-Restoration campaign coincided with the start of an era of agricultural expansion and improvement during which much of the comparatively unproductive common land in the lowland zone was brought into cultivation. The fens of eastern England were drained. The bare chalk uplands of Wessex were broken by the plough. Heathland and wasteland all over England was enclosed and reclaimed. It might be anticipated that the reduction of alleged pests would be a natural side-effect of agricultural expansion—an expansion which, of course, created its own pest problems by unwittingly encouraging species like sparrows and rooks—but it is, at first sight, not easy to understand why campaigns should have been mounted against predatory birds. It is significant, however, that the three main avian targets of persecution besides the grain-eaters were the kite, buzzard, and raven—the smaller raptors such as the kestrel and the sparrowhawk seem to have been killed only casually—and it is to be presumed that these three species had acquired bad reputations as killers of lambs, ducklings and rabbits, and that their presence in large numbers was considered intolerable in a context of increasingly efficient farming. Moreover, their inclusion in the vermin list no doubt gave impetus to the campaign as a whole by involving every countryman who kept chickens—and there could be few who did not—and not merely the landholding classes themselves.

The reasons for the cessation of the campaign against the avian predators may be simpler than those behind its commencement. It may be that in many parishes the churchwardens ceased to pay head-money simply because no kites, buzzards or ravens remained to pay head-money for. More likely, the campaign closed because these three species were no longer sufficiently abundant to be considered major pests whose control it was thought necessary to encourage by subsidy. If persecution on the scale which occurred at Tenterden was widespread, it is little wonder if the campaign folded up for want of material. As Ticehurst remarked, no large raptors' population could long withstand such a drain on its numbers as the hundreds of kites destroyed there in the late seventeenth century. It is in fact doubtful if the Tenterden campaign was typical, but there can be little doubt that in the more accessible and more cultivated lowlands at least, the populations of kites, buzzards and ravens must have been severely depleted and indeed, in many areas, exterminated in the course of the seventeenth and eighteenth centuries.

One further contributory explanation for the cessation of the churchwarden-backed campaign exists. This is that as enclosure of the commons and open fields progressed, so the area of land over which the villager could trap or shoot vermin, or collect eggs or young, decreased—trespassing was hardly encouraged on the enclosed lands, and it is of passing interest to note that an advantage of the sparrow campaign from the landowner's point of view was that it was carried out not on his fields but around the village, and along the laneside hedges.[20] Control of vermin on the enclosed farms and estates fell increasingly on the landowner and, as the eighteenth century progressed, on his gamekeeper. As early as 1768 Robert Smith published *The Universal Directory for Destroying Rats and other Kinds of Fourfooted and Winged Vermin*, in which he suggested methods of trapping buzzards and other predators in order to protect pheasantries and warrens. Firearms were improving (though breach-loaders and percussion caps awaited the nineteenth century) and the art of 'shooting flying' was gaining ground. The closing decades of the eighteenth century marked the development of the keepered estate across the lowland zone of the country. The landed proprietor took upon himself the role relinquished by the churchwarden, and his gamekeeper sought to complete the destruction begun by the villager.

It is doubtful whether it will ever be possible to determine, precisely, what effect the seventeenth- and eighteenth-century persecution had on the population and distribution of the buzzard, or for that matter the kite or raven, though much would emerge from a large-scale and systematic examination of the churchwardens' accounts now gradually accumulating in county and diocesan record offices up and down the country. The task is daunting but offers the prospect of retrieving unique quantitative information about our faunal history. In the meantime it is fair to say that persecution varied in intensity between parishes, and in time. It is clear that many parishes never paid head-money at all for birds of prey. Nevertheless it seems improbable that the generalisations made by Pennant in 1776 and Latham in 1781 can be taken at their face value to imply that the buzzard then remained universally common. Latham's remark, that it was a bird known by everyone, is slightly clouded by his confession that he had not himself seen the eggs of the species. The more critical authors of later county bird histories found little evidence that the buzzard was common in some of the southern and eastern counties at the beginning of the nineteenth century, and it seems likely that it had become, at best, only thinly and patchily distributed over much of the densely settled and farmed lowlands by the second half of the eighteenth. The kite and raven may have been even more local in occurrence. Beyond this it is impossible to conjecture in the absence of more evidence.

The emergence of game preservation as a feature of the management of country estates coincides in time with the heyday of the parliamentary enclosure movement—that is, between about the mid-eighteenth and mid-nineteenth centuries. It was, moreover, in the broad swathe of country from Dorset to Yorkshire, and eastward into East Anglia, where enclosure of the commons and common fields was concentrated, that game rearing and preservation subsequently became most intensive. This is not to suggest that game preservation itself provided a motive for enclosure, but for obvious reasons it became possible only after enclosure. Enclosure and allotment in severalty was prompted largely by the desire of the larger-landed proprietors to break free of the strait-jacket of a more or less communal agriculture in order to benefit from contemporary agricultural innovations. In the process, they expanded and consolidated their estates to form units, which were incidentally of sufficient size to be effective as game reserves. In the west of the country—for example in the South-west Peninsula—where the land had traditionally been held in severalty by small farmers, no such marked movement towards the formation of large estates occurred, and there was consequently less opportunity for the would-be preserver of game.[21]

The new mixed farming of the lowlands, especially in the eastern counties, with its greater variety of crops and its abundant hedgerows separating the new fields laid out at enclosure, no doubt proved an ideal habitat for pheasant and partridge and rabbit. To some extent, too, their deliberate preservation may have been a conscious effort to offset the loss of the formerly almost inexhaustable rough-shooting that had been lost by the reclamation of 'waste' throughout the lowland zone during the eighteenth and nineteenth centuries.[22]

Before the middle of the nineteenth century, shooting was an arduous pastime. Muzzle-loaders were the general rule, and the fields and woods were walked up by the landowner, with perhaps a few friends. Partridge, pheasant, snipe, rabbit and hare, and on the moors, grouse, formed most of the bag, though with many it seems to have been the custom to shoot almost anything—certainly anything unusual or resembling vermin—which was of moderate size and moved. Whatever the bag, however, the sportsman undoubtedly worked hard for it, and a ten- or twelve-hour day was not unusual. With the invention, around 1810, of the copper percussion cap, which led to the development of the central-fire cartridge and to the universal use of the breach-loader, the sport changed. The breach-loader was easily and rapidly loaded and the guns could now stand—with someone to load for them—and await driven birds. The *battue* had arrived.

After the 1850s an increasing area of upland heather, mainly in the Pennines, Southern Uplands, and the central and eastern Highlands of Scotland, came to be managed largely for red grouse. By the 1870s, driving grouse to the guns—and shortly after, in the lowlands, driving pheasants—became common practice. The big shoot adopted many of the aspects of a social rather than strictly sporting occasion. It became the fashionable indulgence of the affluent, and remained so until the outbreak of war in 1914.

The organised driving of game over the guns demanded large numbers of birds, and led inevitably to deliberate rearing of pheasant and partridge, and to the rotational burning of the grouse moors to boost the food source of young heather shoots on which the adult grouse depends. The landowner demanded large bags, and the gamekeeper devoted himself with ruthless single-mindedness to producing them. The period 1880–1914 was the heyday of the pheasant and grouse shoot. Enormous bags were recorded. There are many records of 3,000 pheasants shot in a day, and bags of 1,000 were commonplace. Similarly, on the moor, bags upwards of 1,000 grouse were not infrequent and there are a few records in excess of 2,000. The cost to the predators remaining at this period was correspondingly high.

Man's antipathy towards other predators, arising from his age-old instinctive fear of competition, and nurtured by the subsidised persecution of the sixteenth, seventeenth and early eighteenth centuries, was concentrated into a systematic war of extermination in the nineteenth. Proof of guilt was no necessary precursor to execution. The briefest shadow of suspicion was sufficient. To do him justice, the keeper was—and indeed to some extent still is—often under pressure both from his employer and his pride to produce the maximum bag. He was bound to hit out blindly at anything which might endanger pride or employment, and the sight of a buzzard or sparrowhawk carrying off a pheasant chick would be enough to condemn all predators for all time. 'A hawk as big as a coak-basket must do a tremendous amount of harm,' a nineteenth-century keeper is said to have remarked of the buzzard;[23] and another 'counted the Brown Buzzard as very bad for game and young rabbits, far worse nor the Kites' in his young days in the late eighteenth century,[24] though few nineteenth-century accounts of the buzzard's prey—and there are many—list game birds or their chicks as being taken regularly. The attitude of the landowners may perhaps be summed up by Charles St John:

> In this country . . . we can no more afford to allow hawks and crows, foxes and weasels, to flourish and increase, however picturesque and beautiful they may be, than we could afford to allow poppies or other useless but ornamental wildflowers to overrun our cornfields.

St John had the blood of some of the last pairs of Scottish ospreys on his hands when that was written, and a passage preceding that quoted above describes how to catch buzzards by baiting traps with dead cats. But even St John seems to have had some qualms of conscience: 'I regret, constantly,' he remarked of buzzards, 'to see how rare these birds, and eagles, and many others, are daily becoming, under the influence of traps, poison, and guns.' Crocodile tears indeed![25]

Besides game preservation two other factors contributed to the decline of predator populations. The first was the spread of sheep farming in the uplands after the mid-eighteenth century, which must have increased greatly the pressures on both actual and sup-

Page 49 The buzzard—a robust, compact bird of prey with broad, rounded wings and tail

Page 50 (*above left*) Flight silhouette—soaring; (*above right*) flight silhouette—gliding; (*below*) buzzard habitat—Yarner Wood National Nature Reserve, Devon. Much of Devon supports dense buzzard populations

posed predators of lambs—like buzzards, ravens and eagles—though on the other hand it must also have increased the amount of carrion food available to these species; and the second was the nineteenth-century vogue for amassing collections of stuffed birds and birds' eggs, a practice which often shielded behind a plea of scientific justification.

Much of the uplands had been sheepwalk since the twelfth or thirteenth century. The wealth of the great Cistercian foundations which were raised around the margins of the Pennines, North York Moors, Cumbrian Mountains and the Southern Uplands of Scotland, was based largely on sheep and their wool: nor were the Cistercians the only upland sheep farmers in medieval times. Nonetheless over much of Wales—with the notable exception of the hills inland of the abbey of Strata Florida—and in the Highlands of Scotland, the traditional celtic cattle economy persisted until the eighteenth century. The clearances of the Highland crofting communities, to make way for sheep during the period of mounting wool and mutton prices induced by the French wars, is perhaps the best known episode associated with the conversion of the uplands to sheepwalk. In Scotland the process was only brought to a halt, after about mid-century, by the expansion of grouse moor and deer forest; similarly, in North Wales, extensive areas of upland were retrieved from the sheep, and allotted to the grouse in the second half of the nineteenth century.

It was paradoxical that the interest which natural history engendered in Victorian Britain should in itself assist the keeper in his war against predators. Nineteenth-century ornithology was based largely on the premise that sight records alone were unsatisfactory evidence of a species' occurrence. The bird had to be dead and thus available for subsequent examination. Indisputably, in an age when many comparatively common European birds were still being named and classified, specimens were necessary. To some extent the gun was a substitute for binoculars, and almost by definition the ornithologist was a collector. Scientific necessity, however, far from justified the thousands of collections of birds and birds' eggs which gathered dust in country houses and vicarages in every county. Collecting became a fashionable mania; not of course confined to birds but embracing the buffalo head adorning the wall and the butterfly pinned in the cabinet. Taxidermy, and dealing in mounted specimens and eggs, saw a great boom in the second half of the nineteenth century. The keeper played a key role in satisfying demands for the cabinet. Dealers, taxidermists, and collectors all had their network of keeper contacts who provided both information and specimens. The 'British-killed' bird of prey and its eggs was the *pièce de résistance* of the display room, and the keeper was—naturally—more than willing to oblige. John Wise, writing not long after the middle of the century, summed up the situation in the following passage:

> I am afraid it is too late to protest against the slaughter of our few remaining birds of prey. The eagle and the kite are, to all purposes, extinct, in England, and the peregrine and honey buzzard will soon share their fate. The sight of a large bird now calls out all the raffish guns of a country-side. Ornithologists have, however, themselves to thank. With some honourable exceptions, I know of no one so greedy as a true ornithologist . . . This, I suppose, must be, from the nature of the study, the case.[26]

It is a sad reflection that the collections amassed so assiduously and at the expense of so much life in the nineteenth century are now mostly lost or destroyed. Comparatively few survive to commemorate the mis-directed zeal of their former owners, and many that do are decayed and unlabelled, the pathetic relics of Victorian kleptomania.

The declining fortunes of birds of prey are documented in the considerable ornithological literature of the nineteenth and early twentieth centuries. Apart from numerous general works on British birds, accounts of the history and status of the birds of individual counties began to appear about mid-century, the first being Gurney and Fisher's *Account of the Birds Found in Norfolk*, which appeared in 1846. In 1865, A. G. More published an important paper on the breeding distribution of birds in Britain which documents many of the changes which had occurred during the preceding half century or more.[27] In the last three decades of the century there was a positive flood of local ornithological literature, including from the 1880s the fine Scottish regional *Vertebrate Fauna* series, inspired and largely written by J. A. Harvie-Browne. Accounts of the birds of individual counties also appeared in the *Victoria County History* series, publication of which commenced after 1900, though with a few exceptions these mainly summarised information already published in contemporary county bird books.

Well before the end of the nineteenth century, persecution by keeper and collector had reduced the populations of almost all our predators to negligible proportions over most of the country, had driven many species into relict 'pockets' in remote areas, and had succeeded in actually exterminating a few. It is difficult now to appreciate how large and varied the predator force remained in parts of Britain before the commencement of sustained systematic persecution, but some indication may be found in the records for 'vermin' shot and trapped in some areas of the Scottish Highlands in the years immediately following the arrival of the keeper. Table 1 gives vermin kills on a number of Highland estates. It illustrates both the size and variety of the predator force in the Highlands before the advent of game preservation and large-scale sheep farming, and the appalling destruction which took place with the introduction of these new land uses. The destruction was widely encouraged by landowners who placed a bounty on the heads of many of the supposedly more noxious species. Eagles in particular attracted large rewards: one guinea and ten shillings each respectively were paid for the 171 adults and 53 young and eggs destroyed on the Duchess of Sutherland's estates between 1831 and 1834.[28] Few areas of the lowlands of Britain would have possessed so large a predator element in their fauna by the nineteenth century, but the destruction of what remained was no less intensive than on the Highland estates.

The kite was scarce by the 1850s, and by the end of the century had been reduced to a small nucleus in mid-Wales, where it still survives. The raven, which had shared with the kite and the

TABLE I

Scottish Vermin Kills[29]

LOCALITY	*Birds of prey (except Eagles)*	*Eagles*	*Ravens and Crows (including Magpies)*	*Foxes*	*Wild cats, Pole-cats, Martens*	*Stoats and Weasels*	*Badgers*	*Otters*	*Owls*
Braemar, Crathie, Glenmuick, Tulloch and Glengarden parishes, Aberdeen, 1776–86	2,520	70	1,347	634	44 (wild cats only)				
Langwell and Sandside estates, Sutherland, 1819–26	1,115	295 adults; 60 young & eggs	4,609	546					
Sutherland estate, Sutherland, 1831–4	1,055	171 adults; 53 young & eggs	2,675 (936 Ravens)	193	901			263	
Glengarry estate, Inverness, 1837–40	1,754	42	1,906 (475 Ravens)	11	550	301	67	48	109

buzzard the brunt of sixteenth- and seventeenth-century persecution, was confined to the less inhabited upland areas by the end of the nineteenth century. The honey buzzard, which once bred widely, though never commonly, in England, retained only a precarious toehold in the south of England by the 1880s. Both osprey and sea eagle had been lost by the end of the first decade of this century: indeed, no more than scattered pairs of either species had bred—in Scotland—since the 1840s. Golden eagles, which formerly bred in northern England, North Wales and Ireland, were by the 1870s reduced to a relict population in the central and western Highlands and Western Isles. Hen harriers had been reduced to surviving pockets in the Orkneys and Outer Hebrides, and marsh harriers to a few pairs in southern and eastern England by 1900. Even kestrels and sparrowhawks had become uncommon over much of the lowlands when the present century dawned. The pattern is much the same with the predatory mammals. Polecat, pine marten and wild cat had all been reduced to small relict populations in remote areas of Scotland and Wales by the 1870s or 1880s. Only the smaller and rather more elusive animals like the weasel and stoat, and the fox—preserved for hunting—remained widespread.

The buzzard had gone from most of the lowland zone of Britain by the middle of the nineteenth century. A. G. More summarised its distribution thus in 1865: 'By no means common, and nearly exterminated in the eastern and midland counties of England. Still breeds regularly in several parts of the west and north of England and in Scotland, where it has a better chance of escaping the vigilance of the gamekeeper.'[30] More was the first to attempt the systematic study of bird distribution, and he lists under each species the subprovinces (usually groups of two or three counties) from which it was recorded as breeding by his network of correspondents. From More's data, amplified by contemporary county bird histories and bird lists (often, incidentally, prepared by his correspondents), it is possible to reconstruct the breeding distribution of the buzzard in the 1860s in some detail. This has been attempted in Fig 1. Fig 2 shows the species breeding distribution in 1915 after a further half-century of persecution and immediately before the pressure was lifted. Both figures agree, in essentials, with reconstructions attempted by N. W. Moore.[31]

Figs 1 and 2 are eloquent enough in themselves, though that for the earlier date needs to be accepted with some reserve because reliable observers were then thin on the ground. In the lowlands, it shows relict populations in West Suffolk, Lincolnshire, Sussex, Hampshire, Dorset and Wiltshire, but there may well have been pockets surviving elsewhere. The last breeding record for West Suffolk was in 1874 (inevitably one of the adults was shot by a keeper), whilst attempted breeding was recorded there in 1875.[32]

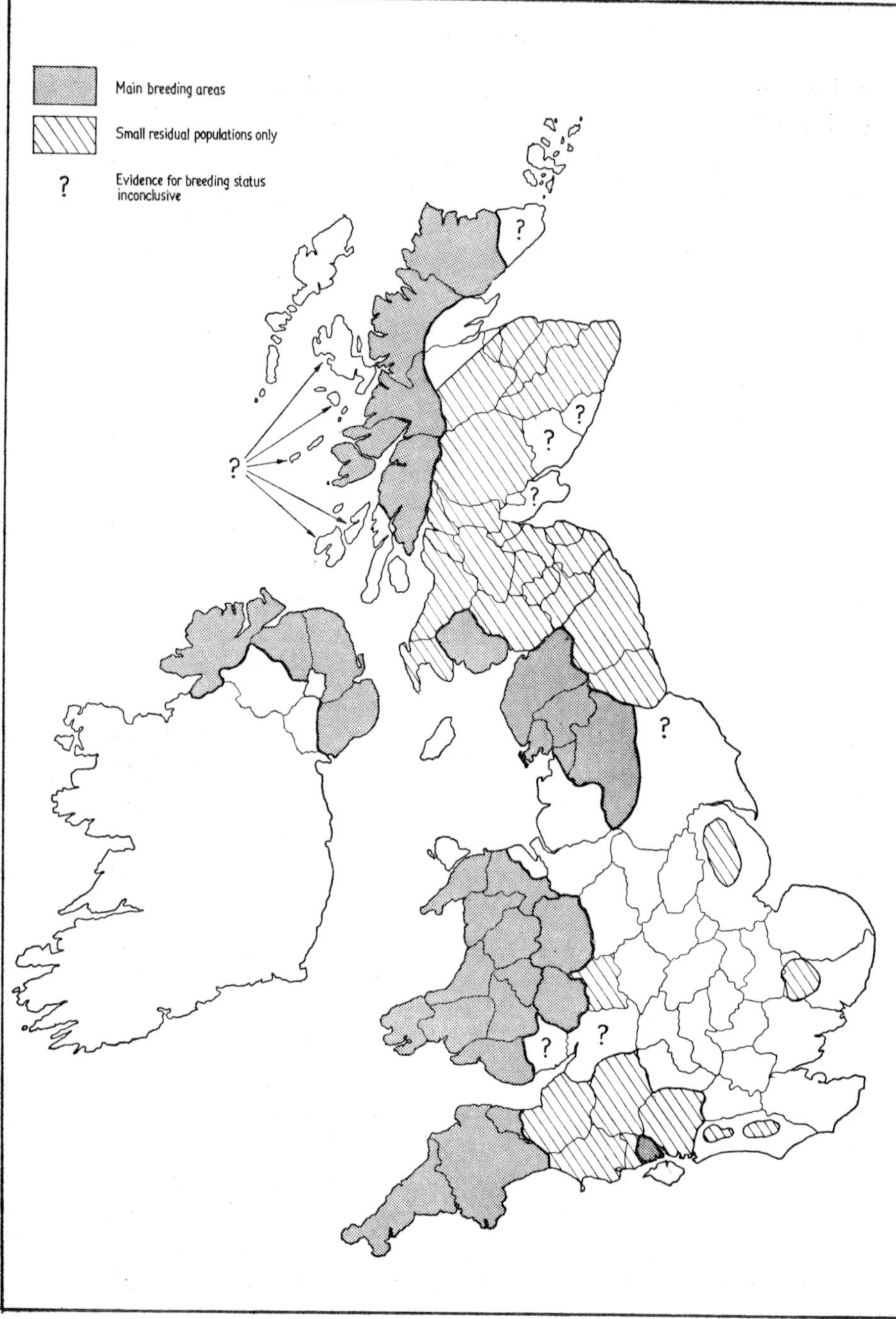

1 Breeding distribution of the buzzard in the British Isles in c1865

In Lincolnshire, breeding was recorded as late as 1888.[33] In Sussex, James Walpole-Bond considered (mainly on the evidence of an old keeper) that a small breeding population survived in the Ashdown Forest area until about 1882 and probably also in the extreme west of the county until about the same date.[34] Scattered breeding pairs appear to have survived on the chalklands of Hampshire, Dorset and Wiltshire until late in the century,[35] whilst in the New Forest, in Hampshire, the tide may have turned somewhat in favour of the buzzard a decade or more before the close of the century through the intervention of an enlightened administrator.

In the upland zone the buzzard's strongholds in 1865 were the South-west Peninsula, Wales, Lakeland and the western Highlands of Scotland. Eslewhere numbers were small. In the extreme north, in Ross, Sutherland and Caithness, the buzzard had probably never been common, but in the central and eastern Highlands, in the Scottish Lowlands and Southern Uplands, and in Northumberland and the Pennines, the keeper and sheep farmer had undoubtedly been responsible for depleting its numbers, and indeed, it is probable that its distribution as shown on Fig 1 masks widespread local extinctions in many counties. Around Abernethy Forest in the Spey valley in Inverness-shire, for example, the buzzard was reported to have become extinct around 1850. In Kintyre, Argyll, it was exterminated about the same time.[36]

There is no evidence that the buzzard ever bred in the Orkneys, Shetlands or—until the present century—the Outer Hebrides, and the evidence for breeding on most of the Inner Hebrides until late in the nineteenth century is inconclusive. In Ireland the buzzard was recorded in 1849 as breeding in the four northern counties of Donegal, Londonderry, Antrim and Down, and also further south in Tipperary and Wexford.[37] In the 1850s it seems to have become confined to the north, where it occurred 'in limited numbers along the basaltic precipices of the coast'.[38] There is insufficient information from which to reconstruct or deduce the distribution of the buzzard in Ireland before the middle of the nineteenth century, but it is not unlikely that it was once widespread and that the mid-century references are to a relict population. It was finally dislodged

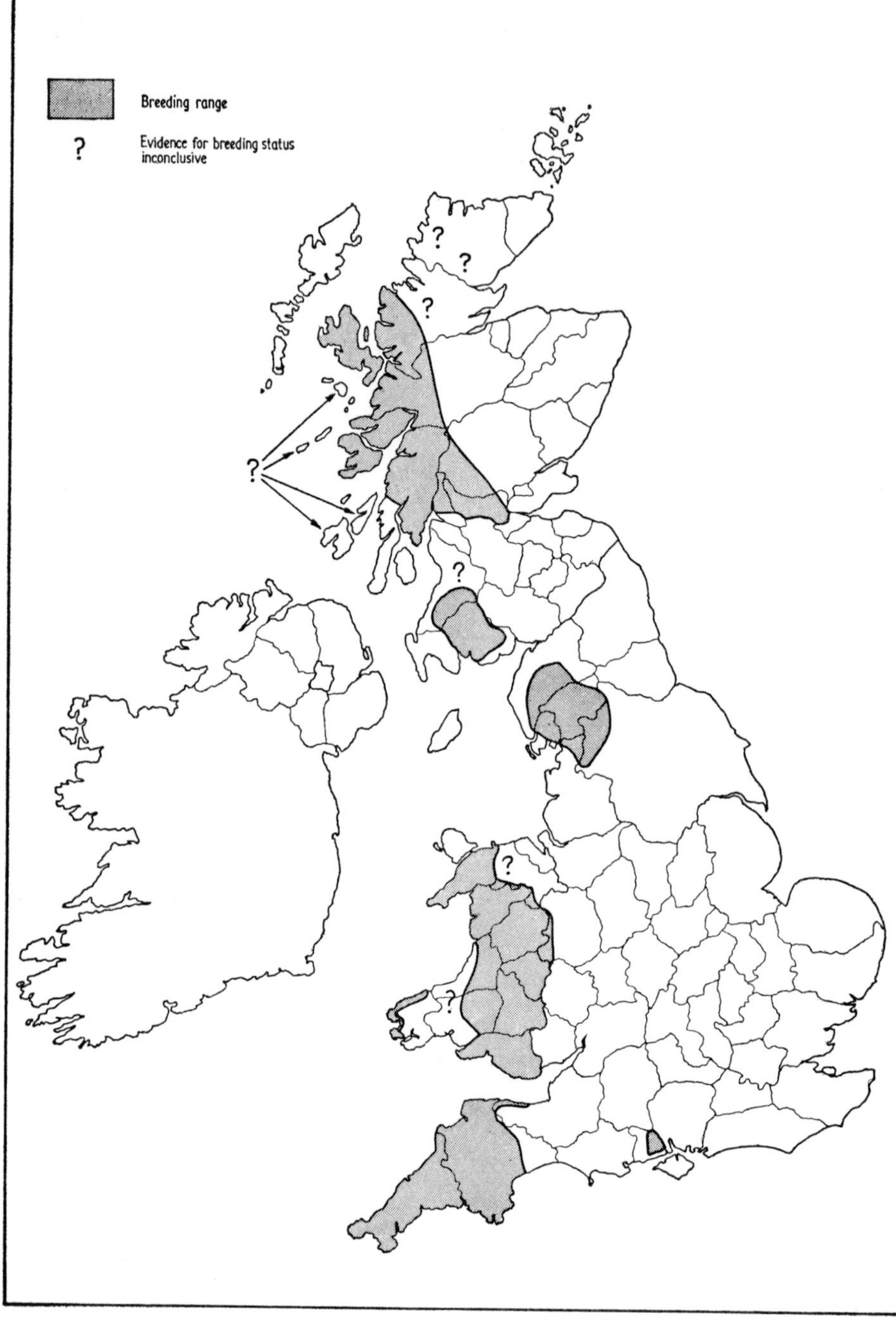

2 Breeding distribution of the buzzard in the British Isles in 1915

from the north coast in the 1880s: it probably last bred in Donegal in 1883 and in Derry in 1885 or 1886, though a pair returned to Antrim one year between 1905 and 1915.[39]

The buzzard's strongholds in 1865 were, by 1915, the species' only breeding areas in Britain—Cornwall, Devon and the Exmoor coast in the South-west Peninsula; the Pembrokeshire coast and the mountain districts in Wales; the Cumbrian dome in north-west England; Kirkcudbrightshire and Ayrshire and the western Highlands and Inner Isles in Scotland. In the lowland zone a breeding population of buzzards remained in a single outlying district—the New Forest in Hampshire. Over much of this residual breeding range the actual population of buzzards had become small. By 1894 only six pairs remained on the coastal cliffs of Pembrokeshire.[40] So far as can be deduced from the literature, there were probably no more than about thirty pairs in Lakeland by the beginning of this century,[41] and fewer still in Kirkcudbright and Ayrshire.[42] The largest populations persisted in Devon and Cornwall, in parts of central Wales, and in Argyll, western Inverness-shire, and some of the Inner Hebrides. It seems uncertain if buzzards were still hanging on in the more northern counties of Ross, Cromarty and Sutherland by 1915, or indeed, by the turn of the century. In 1887, Harvie-Browne and Buckley could cite only one breeding record which 'came under their observation' in Sutherland, Caithness and western Cromarty,[43] whilst in 1904 Harvie-Browne and Macpherson described the buzzard as 'very rare' in Ross 'and further north' as a result of persecution—on one estate in Wester Ross 86 buzzards, 'almost the whole crop', were killed between 1877 and 1902.[44]

Only in the most remote, inaccessible, or unkeepered areas, or (rarely) where the landowner was heretically enlightened enough to tolerate predators, did the buzzard survive by 1915. The first Wild Birds' Protection Act had been passed in 1880, and though the buzzard was not included in the schedules of protected species, the Act authorised the alteration of the schedules by ministerial orders made for individual counties—usually at the request of the county council—and most of the supplementary orders made around the turn of the century extended protection to the buzzard and its eggs —and, indeed, to other raptors as well. The pole-trap, the chief means of catching buzzards (and a particularly cruel contrivance) was made illegal in England and Wales in 1904. The law as such, however, afforded little protection. It was (and in this context still is) difficult to enforce, and affected the prejudices of few keepers.

The Hon Gerald Lascelles was a heretic who was as interested in preserving buzzards as he was pheasants, and it was at least partly because of him that a breeding population of buzzards survived the height of the persecution era in the geographical isolation of the New Forest. The forest, it is true, was not managed for game preservation during the period of the buzzard's decline, but nevertheless the species suffered there from the collectors, assisted, until 1880, by the Crown keepers. Until the 1860s the buzzard appears to have remained numerous. John Wise, in 1863, recorded that it bred 'in nearly all the old woods, but is becoming scarce',[45] and in the following two decades many clutches and specimens of adults were taken in the forest. In 1880 Lascelles was appointed Deputy Surveyor of the New Forest, a post which carried complete responsibility for the management of this large Crown estate. The situation which he found and his attitude towards it can be best described in his own words:

> . . . everything in the shape of rare birds that they [the keepers] could get hold of they regarded as perquisites. With some trouble I discovered the Southampton birdstuffer who was in the habit of regularly paying 3/6d per head for all the kingfishers he could get. Everything in the shape of a bird of prey was, of course, looked upon as vermin, killed, and if possible sold . . .

Under Lascelles' administration a new policy of wildlife conservation emerged:

> Full instructions for all keepers were carefully drawn up . . . I had in view the object of preserving all the fauna of the Forest of every kind

> . . . I had to make my men understand that I desired the same care taken of the nest of a buzzard or fern-owl as of a pheasant . . . and there was to be no killing of any birds save a few scheduled ones. Of course these were rather novel ideas to some of the men, but, after a change or two had been made among them, they all settled down well in their work, and in some cases became keen and intelligent observers of wildlife.[46]

Hardly anything more novel than not shooting a buzzard could have occurred to a countryman in 1880. Compare Lascelles' attitude with that prevailing on the Mottisfont estate, only a few miles north of the New Forest, where the late Colonel Richard Meinertzhagen spent his boyhood, from 1884 to 1900:

> Things are better now, but when we were at Mottisfont no kestrel or owl or hedgehog was ever allowed to live; keepers would loaf about with a gun shooting everything big, including woodpeckers. Many estates had exterminated hawks, owls, rooks, jackdaws, herons, little grebe, moorhen, coot, water-voles, badgers, squirrel, and hedgehogs under the impression that game birds alone should be allowed to live.[47]

The Hon Gerald Lascelles pursued his policy of wildlife conservation until he retired in 1915. Not only does this seem to have had more immediate effects but it also fostered a tradition of conservation among the forest keepers which remains strong today.

Thus, the buzzard survived in the New Forest whilst it was exterminated on the encircling chalklands; though it must remain doubtful if the population in the forest was anything like as substantial in 1915 as it has become since. A few local memories can reach back to Lascelles' day and recall some of the buzzard breeding sites which he took pains to protect against collectors—sometimes with the most diabolical contrivances affixed to the tree—but there is nobody who remembers just how many buzzards there were to protect.

Chapter Three

RECOVERY

1915–1971

Large-scale game preservation came to an abrupt halt with the outbreak of World War I, and predatory birds and mammals responded rapidly to the cessation of trapping and shooting. The numbers of buzzards increased and there was a marked eastward extension of their breeding range, at least in England. This phase of expansion continued at a reduced rate throughout the twenties and thirties, accelerating again during World War II when once again the gamekeeper departed from the countryside. To some extent, no doubt, the recovery of the buzzard and some other predators was assisted by a progressively more tolerant attitude among landowners and gamekeepers; by legal protection; by the fall-off in the number of agricultural workers, many of whom would be likely to shoot or trap buzzards in at least a casual fashion; and by the increasing commuter and retired element in the countryside, whose response to nature was often more enlightened than that of the indigenous countryman. It is doubtful, however, if these factors contributed as significantly to the buzzard's expansion during and between the wars as did the simple fact that there were fewer keepers (and fewer full-time keepers) on the ground than formerly. In particular, it would be naïve to assume that legal protection in itself affected the attitudes of those who reared game. 'Just so long as the eggs and skins may be sold, and just so long as the gamekeeper is permitted to carry a gun at all times . . . so will the slaughter continue. The so-called protection afforded these birds is useless,' protested one writer in 1914,[1] and there is little evidence to suggest a fundamental change in attitudes towards predators after the war.

The phase of expansion continued until the advent of myxomatosis. Dr N. W. Moore's survey of the buzzard in Britain carried out in 1954, clearly demonstrated that there remained at that time an adverse correlation between the distribution of gamekeepers and the distribution of buzzards in Britain. Thereafter the relationship between the buzzard and the keeper becomes complicated by the introduction of other adverse, or potentially adverse, factors—myxomatosis, and the agricultural use of organochlorine pesticides.

After 1915, food production had, perforce, to take precedence over game rearing and, as important, the armed services drained the countryside of gamekeepers. Game preservation recommenced after the war, of course, but mostly on a comparatively modest scale. It is beyond the scope of this book to examine the social upheavals of the time, but for various reasons the great estates were starting to break up and there was less money for rural investment. Few landowners could now afford large staffs of gamekeepers, nor could they afford to place pheasants before the interests of their tenant farmers, who now had some experience of farming without the inconvenient restrictions imposed by landowners for the benefit of the game. Moreover, few landowners could any longer afford to rear game in the massive nineteenth-century style simply for the entertainment of themselves and their guests. Game preservation had, increasingly, to pay its way as an estate enterprise alongside farming, forestry and fishing. The guns now paid for their shooting. The syndicate began to emerge as a rural institution.

Syndicate shoots varied in nature in the years between the wars. At one end of the spectrum might be the rough shoot with, perhaps, a part-time keeper rearing a handful of pheasants to supplement the bag, and ritualistically shooting the odd buzzard or sparrowhawk; at the other, the fashionable grouse moor where anything resembling a predator was shot or trapped. Whatever its scale, however, management remained in the hands of the landowner, and in order to give the maximum return on investment there thus tended to be strong constraints on the size of the keeping staff employed. The syndicate was given something of a boost during the Depression years when many estates were thrown back on the shoot as a proportionately more important source of income than farming. World War II saw a repetition in the countryside of the events which followed 1915, and though after 1945 the shoot became gradually re-established as an important enterprise on most estates and large farms (if there was by then a real distinction) in the lowlands, and the grouse moor an important form of land use in the uplands, the persecution of predators, although still intensive in some areas and on individual properties, never achieved the proportions of the era before 1915.

World War I saw not only substantial increases in the buzzard populations of the strongholds in the west, but also the recovery of much lost ground, albeit much of it only temporarily. Buzzards spread back into Somerset, Dorset, Gloucestershire, and as far east as Oxfordshire in the south; into the Welsh border counties and west Midlands; and into parts of the Pennines. An eastward spread seems also to have started in Scotland, though it is inadequately documented. Much of this regained ground was lost again after the war when the gamekeeper returned to the land. F. C. R. Jourdain recorded the wartime resurgence of predatory birds and crows in the southern counties thus:

> Another noteworthy episode was the sudden increase of Hawks and Crows which followed on the drainage of our man-power during the war and the cessation of game preserving. For a season or two the Kestrels increased enormously . . . Buzzards appeared in summer in the larger woods in many parts of our southern counties and showed signs of recolonising their ancient haunts. But here, unlike the more inaccessible parts of England and Wales, the change has not been permanent, and a few years of heavy shooting and trapping has brought back the conditions to much the same as in pre-war times, though the number of men employed is probably rather less.[2]

Despite the post-war setback to its expansion, the pressure on buzzard populations was never so ruthlessly reasserted as to prevent, between the wars, the gradual consolidation of breeding populations on much ground recolonised initially between 1915 and 1919. Indeed, the 1930s appear to have witnessed a definite expansion of the buzzard's breeding range. In the south, Wiltshire was colonised by a scatter of pairs, associated with the larger woodlands of the county, during the 1930s: as early as 1933 there were reports of pairs or single birds from eight localities in the county during the breeding season, in two of which—both on the Hampshire/Wiltshire border close to the New Forest—breeding was confirmed.[3] Dorset, colonised during World War I but evidently cleared of buzzards again afterwards, was colonised again from east Devon, and probably also the New Forest, in the late 1930s.[4] In Somerset, the spread which had begun after 1915 continued—first over Exmoor and the Brendon Hills and Quantocks, and subsequently across the remainder of the county.[5] Further west, in Devon —always a stronghold of the buzzard—the increase which had commenced in 1915 continued throughout the inter-war period. In 1929 a census by the newly-formed Devon Bird Watching and Preservation Society enabled them to estimate the total buzzard population of the county as about one thousand birds. By then many districts of Devon from which buzzards had been exterminated before 1915 had been recolonised. The Tavy valley below Denham Bridge, where buzzards were only exceptionally seen before 1915, was first recolonised in 1918 and by 1929 was reported to carry a dense breeding population.[6]

In northern England and in Scotland, the eastward spread appears to have been less successful—or, for Scotland at least, conceivably merely less well recorded—than in the south. The drier, more eastern hill country was—and is—widely managed as grouse moor rather than sheepwalk or (in the Highlands) deer forest, and it is probable that here persecution remained intensive between the wars. In northern England the buzzard's breeding range remained virtually confined to the Cumbrian mountains. During World War I, breeding had taken place in Northumberland for the first time for several decades, but the birds failed to survive long into the post-war years.[7] In the Southern Uplands of Scotland the buzzard remained confined mainly to its strongholds in Kirkcudbrightshire and Ayrshire, though a gradual colonisation of Dumfriesshire began in the 1920s. In the Highlands, too, expansion seems to have been slow, though by the late 1930s buzzards were breeding as far east as the Spey valley. In the western Highlands and Inner Hebrides—as in that other stronghold, Devon—numbers increased considerably, and during the 1930s colonisation of the Outer Hebrides commenced[8]—evidently for the first time in the recorded history of the species, for Harvie-Browne and Buckley's *Vertebrate Fauna of the Outer Hebrides*, published in 1888 gives no authentic information about the species, and I have been unable to find any earlier reference to breeding in the Outer Isles. In Ireland, a pair bred on the Antrim coast in 1933 and attempted to do so again the following year—the first recorded breeding since the 1880s if one excludes a rather vague record of a pair breeding in Antrim in one year between 1905 and 1915. There appear, however, to be no further records of breeding in Ireland until after World War II.[9]

The ornithological literature—and especially the annual reports of county ornithological societies—is unanimous in recording the expansion of buzzard populations—and indeed of many other raptors—during and after World War II. By the early 1950s the buzzard was probably more numerous and more widespread in Britain than it had been for a hundred years or so. Fig 3 is reproduced (with some minor amendments) from Norman Moore's account of his 1954 buzzard survey,[10] and shows the species' distribution in that year, together with a crude assessment of its population density. It will be seen that in the lowlands the buzzard spread as far east as Northamptonshire, Buckinghamshire, Surrey and East Sussex. It was firmly re-established in the Welsh border counties and in Gloucestershire, Wiltshire, Somerset and Dorset. It had spread into Staffordshire and Derbyshire. In the north of England and in the Southern Uplands of Scotland, however, it remained confined to the western counties: Northumberland, Durham, most of Yorkshire and Lancashire away from the

Page 67 (*above*) Snowdonia. In hill country buzzards achieve dense breeding populations mainly in wooded valleys; (*below*) the New Forest, Hampshire—112 square miles which supports between 33 and 37 pairs of buzzards

Page 68 (*above*) Buzzard at carrion rabbit; (*below*) contestants for prey—buzzard and carrion crow. Compare the buzzard's plumage with the bird shown on p 49

Cumbrian mountains, and Roxburgh, Selkirk, Lanark, Peebles, Berwick and the Lothians remained uncolonised. In the Scottish Highlands it had recovered vast areas of ground lost during the nineteenth century. In Ireland it had recolonised the Antrim coast.

For the most part the population densities on Fig 3 are shown for counties, and the figure inevitably presents a comparatively crude representation of the buzzard's distribution. Over much of its distribution in the Scottish Highlands and in Wales, there remained considerable tracts of country with few or no buzzards because of persecution, lack of nest sites, paucity of prey, or a combination of all three. In the lowland counties, shown on Fig 3 as carrying the least dense populations, there was little more than a thin scatter of pairs. Warwickshire, Worcestershire and Staffordshire between them, for example, in 1954,[11] held only 25 pairs, of which 15 were known to have bred, and only 5 pairs were recorded from the whole of Sussex in the same year.[12] In addition to the counties shown as carrying breeding pairs in 1954 at least 1 pair may have been breeding in south Lancashire,[13] whilst a pair bred at Eaton Park in Cheshire the following year.[14]

The handful of breeding pairs in Surrey in 1954 may have been partially derived from an apparently successful reintroduction into the county a little more than a decade earlier. In 1939 seven young buzzards were removed from nests in Wales, and after fledging in an aviary at Witley Park in Surrey, six of them, together with a four-year-old adult, were liberated. In the following spring the remaining young bird and a second adult were released in the same locality. During the breeding season of 1940 at least five birds were present in the area and in spring 1941 two nests were found, from one of which two young were reared, the other being deserted because of nearby felling. In addition a third pair was present in the area and was thought to have bred successfully.[15] The subsequent outcome of the Witley Park experiment is obscured by the species' wartime expansion—to which it is unlikely to have made more than a minor contribution—and one cannot but feel that its ultimate success would also have depended on freedom from persecution.

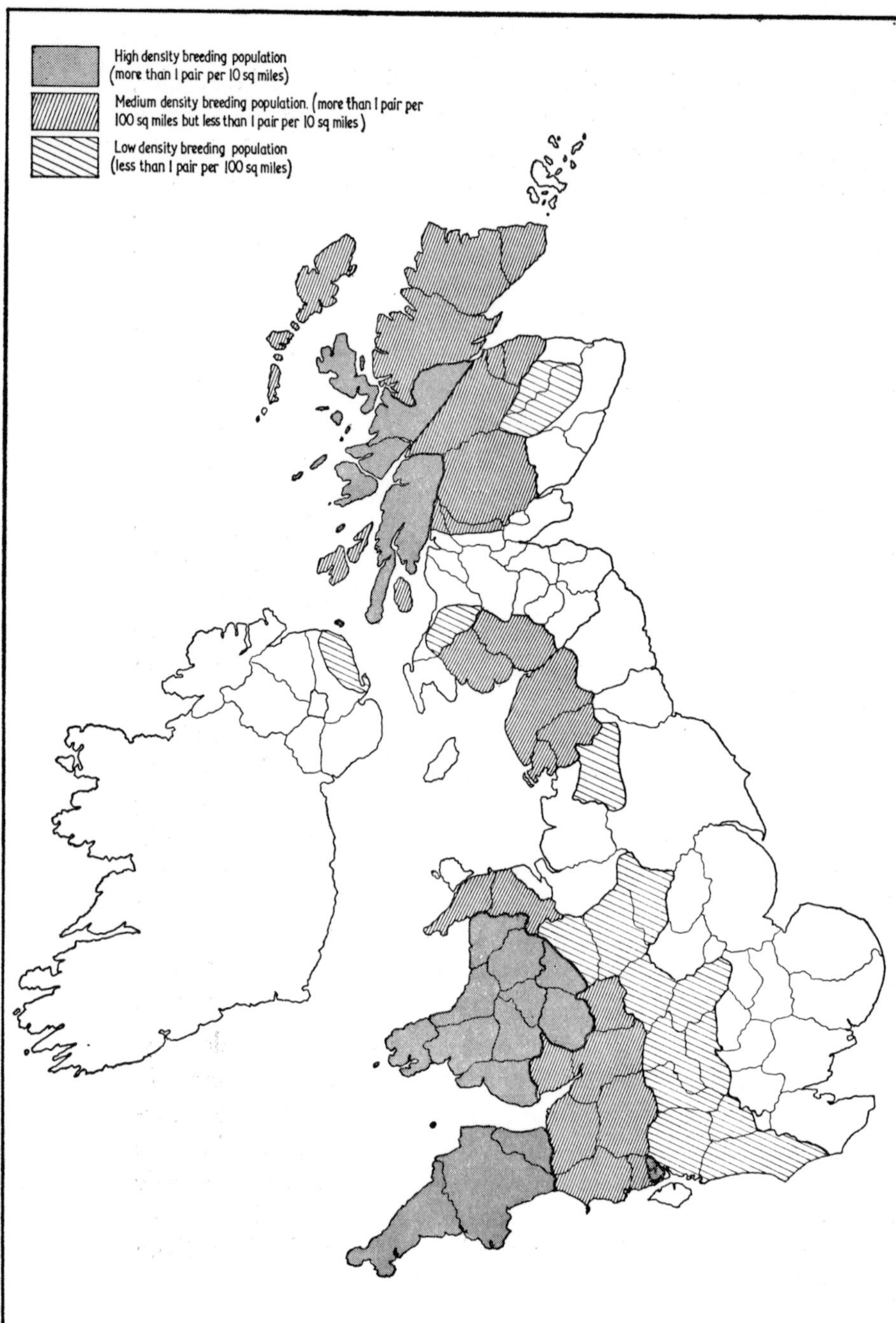

3 **Breeding distribution of the buzzard in the British Isles in 1954 (after N. W. Moore, *Brit Birds*, 50 (1957), 188)**

In the Wessex chalklands, the buzzard continued to increase after World War I, despite renewed persecution. In Dorset, W. J. Ashford found about twenty breeding pairs in 1947, and considerably more were thought to have been present in the county. Both then, and in subsequent years, the Dorset buzzards were recorded as being persecuted by both keepers and poultry farmers, and in 1949 it was noted that 'due largely to human persecution, apparently, the spectacular recovery of this species in Dorset in the past decade shows signs of a check'. The same source cites several known instances in which nests were destroyed.[16] The population in 1954, however, was certainly no less and probably substantially more than twenty pairs. A comparable number were probably breeding in the neighbouring county of Wiltshire[17] and a thinner scatter of pairs over the Hampshire chalk where keepering was particularly intensive.[18]

Turning to my own buzzard study area, the New Forest, printed references to buzzards are few and vague until the 1950s. The earliest date for which there is a published population figure is 1940, when according to Edwin Cohen, author of the most recent county bird history, 'J. B. Watson, a reliable and cautious observer, estimated that about ten pairs were breeding in the Forest'. Cohen thought this figure had probably doubled by the early 1950s.[19] The manuscript notes of the late Mr B. J. Ringrose, covering the period 1927–35,[20] shed a somewhat different light on the buzzard's status in the forest between the wars. Ringrose's notes contain repeated references to pairs or nests at thirteen localities in the north and west of my study area in every year between 1928 and 1935. Of these localities all but one carried nesting pairs between 1962 and 1971, whilst I recorded only two additional breeding pairs in the area during the same period, which suggests that the breeding population in the late 1920s and early 1930s was little different from that of today. If the memories of the older forest keepers are accurate—they are certainly consistent one with another—this picture held good for the forest as a whole during the three decades preceding 1954. Some further evidence is provided by the manuscript notes of the late Mr Peter Day, which confirm that the buzzard was numerous in the forest during the 1940s. In 1943, and again in 1947, he refers to nests, young on the wing, or pairs of adults, at seven localities around Burley Lodge, where he lived, all of which carried breeding pairs between 1962 and 1971.[21] Such evidence as there is, therefore, suggests that the buzzard population of the New Forest has changed little since the 1920s or before, thought it is not inconceivable that the area shared the national build-up of population which occurred in the decade or so before myxomatosis.

In its strongholds in the west—and especially in the South-west Peninsula, in Wales and in western Scotland—the buzzard had, by 1954, become easily the most common raptor, sometimes achieving population densities in excess of 2 pairs per square mile in the most favourable habitats.[22] On the island of Skomer, off the Pembrokeshire coast, a density of 7·08 pairs per square mile (8 pairs on 722 acres) was recorded in 1954,[23] the highest recorded population density for the species. Pembrokeshire, too, provides some idea of the scale of the buzzard's increase in the west during this century if we compare R. M. Lockley's figure of 120 pairs in the county in 1949 with M. A. Mathew's figure of 6 pairs in 1894.[24]

Finally, buzzards returned to Ireland in 1951. By 1953 3 pairs were breeding on Rathlin Island and another on the mainland cliffs of Antrim. In 1954 the population stood at 10 pairs.[25] By the early 1960s, however, they had gone once again, as indeed they were to go from other outlying fringes of the buzzard's range in Britain, this time, apparently, the result of changes in food supply rather than changes in man's behaviour towards predators.

The buzzard's distribution in Britain today (1972) is little different from that given by Norman Moore for 1954 (Fig 3), though a number of counties then on the eastern fringe of the species' range in the English Midlands and southern counties would today no longer qualify for inclusion on the map. A straightforward comparison of mapped distribution in 1954 and 1972, however, would mask significant and interesting events. The period between these two dates saw the cessation of the eastward spread of the buzzard in England, the temporary disappearance, once more, of the small breeding population on the Antrim coast of Ireland, and reductions in some breeding populations elsewhere. Only in the Scottish Highlands does the pre-1954 spread seem to have continued. The main factor involved in checking the buzzard's continued success during the 1954–72 period was probably the spread of myxomatosis among the rabbit population during the mid-1950s, but other local declines may possibly be attributable to organochlorine pesticide contamination and increasing persecution by keepers and poultry farmers and shepherds. It is often difficult to distinguish the relative effects of these various factors in a given area, but an attempt is made to consider them separately in the following pages.

Although Willughby noted that the buzzard was 'a great destroyer of conies' as long ago as 1676,[26] it was not until the present century that the rabbit became inextricably associated with the buzzard in the minds of countrymen and ornithologists: few nineteenth-century accounts of the buzzard's diet mention the rabbit as a particularly important prey animal, though most include it among lists of other prey species. This accords well with the known history of the rabbit in Britain. The rabbit only became a widespread agricultural pest in Britain in the latter part of the nineteenth century. Like the house sparrow, skylark and rook (among other species) its population expanded—one might better say exploded—in response to increased food supply made available by agricultural improvement. Witness man bringing about his own pest problem! By the late 1930s the rabbit population of Britain was estimated to be about 50 million, and by the early 1950s the number was thought to have risen to between 60 million and 100 million.[27] Most authors agree that in the two or three decades preceding myxomatosis the rabbit—and especially young rabbits, in late spring and summer—formed the most important single source of food for buzzards in Britain. Although, surprisingly, there is little quantitative evidence to support this view, it is nonetheless true that the decimation of the rabbit by myxomatosis in the 1950s had a profound effect on the buzzard.

The existence of the virus *Myxomatosis cuniculus* had been known since the end of the nineteenth century, and between the wars various unsuccessful or at least inconclusive attempts were made to spread it among wild rabbit populations, both in Europe and in Australia. In the 1940s, however, the importance of the rabbit flea (and in damp climates, mosquitoes) as a vector was recognised, and in the early 1950s myxomatosis was successfully introduced into rabbit populations in France. A devastating epidemic commenced, and in the summer of 1953 the disease appeared in south-east England. During the ensuing two years it spread throughout the country, widely assisted by the deliberate introduction of affected rabbits into disease-free areas. By the end of the winter of 1955–6 the rabbit had been virtually eliminated from much of the country: myxomatosis achieved an incredible 99 per cent kill in the rabbit population. By 1958, however, it was already becoming clear that residual populations were surviving myxomatosis. In the decade or so that has elapsed since, there has been a widespread recovery of the rabbit population, though the virus has become endemic, and appears to exert a control on the rise of rabbit populations beyond a certain limit.[28]

In 1954, 1956 and 1957, Norman Moore organised British Trust for Ornithology sponsored surveys of buzzard populations, one of the main objects of which was to determine the buzzard's response to the virtual loss of the rabbit. The results of the surveys suggested that after a normal breeding season in 1954, there was a great decrease in breeding activity the following year in all regions where rabbits had become rare or extinct. Many, perhaps most pairs, failed to breed at all. Breeding activity was normal in areas where rabbits either remained unaffected by myxomatosis or had never been abundant. In 1956 there was much less breeding than in 1954, but about twice as much as in 1955. The buzzard population was reportedly smaller than in 1954.[29] These general conclusions were based partly on the subjective opinions of observers, and one has to remember that any survey of this kind inevitably involves a certain amount of question-begging. There would in fact appear to have been considerable local and regional variation in the buzzard's response to myxomatosis.

In many areas which in 1954 carried the densest buzzard populations, notably the South-west Peninsula and parts of Wales, the output of young appears temporarily to have become much reduced, whilst population decreases of 50 per cent or more were reported, as the density of the buzzard population readjusted to the lower prey-biomass. It is no coincidence that it was in these areas that the rabbit had also been most abundant before myxomatosis, presumably thus enabling the buzzard to achieve exceptional densities.[30]

Peter Dare, who studied a population of buzzards in the Postbridge area of Dartmoor during the critical period, observed that in 1956, the first breeding season after the arrival of myxomatosis on the moor, they adjusted to the change of diet much more rapidly than had the birds of lowland Devon in 1955. Most of the Postbridge pairs succeeded in rearing single young birds on a diet mainly of voles, whilst one pair, which occupied a territory which included a small but healthy rabbit warren, reared two young on a mixed rabbit-and-vole diet. Dare remarked that the breeding season throughout the remainder of Devon was less successful than on Dartmoor in 1956, though certainly an improvement on 1955.[31] In the Barnstaple area, however, C. G. Manning reported that in 1956 the population had been reduced to about one-third of the 1954 population, and that few pairs had attempted to breed. Of 3 occupied nests found, 2 clutches of only 1 egg each were lost during incubation; and a third clutch of 2 eggs hatched successfully, though only 1 young was reared.[32] Similar reports of nest failures were a feature of the immediate post-myxomatosis years.

On Skomer, which it will be remembered had carried no less than 8 pairs of buzzards on its 722 acres in 1954, there was a dramatic fall in the population after myxomatosis reached the island. This seems to have occurred in the winter of 1954–5, but it appears to have spread slowly, and enough rabbits survived into the spring to support the dense buzzard population. By the following spring, however, scarcely any rabbits remained and only two pairs of buzzards were present—and these succeeded in rearing only a single young bird between them. 1957 saw a recovery of the buzzard population to five pairs and it has remained at between three and five pairs since, though breeding success has been diminished: in 1960, when the rabbit population was again very low, no young at all were reared, and only one of the four pairs present attempted to breed; and again after the cold winter of 1962–3 there was a total breeding failure. Davis and Saunders, in discussing the failure of the Skomer buzzards to regain their former numbers despite a general recovery in the numbers of rabbits, suggested that sublethal contamination by organochlorine pesticide residues might have become a contributory cause. There is no evidence to support this, however, and the explanation is more likely to be simply that although the rabbit has recovered, it fails to achieve the superabundance necessary to support 8 pairs of buzzards on 722 acres before myxomatosis intervenes once again.[33] The events on Skomer mirror those on many small offshore islands where rabbits tended to be exeptionally abundant before 1954.

Further features of the myxomatosis episode were the dwindling away of the small Antrim population, until by the early 1960s it was doubtful if any were breeding at all; and the retraction of the buzzard's range from some of the counties in southern and midland England which had been most recently colonised. The scatter of pairs in Derbyshire, Northamptonshire, Oxfordshire, Buckinghamshire, and probably those in Berkshire, disappeared in the mid-1950s, and the numbers in some other adjoining counties where the populations had also been small—Worcestershire, Warwickshire, Staffordshire, north Hampshire and Surrey—were reduced to a precarious level. This decrease at the eastern margin of the buzzard's range was not necessarily the outcome of myxomatosis in the areas involved. It is likely that to counter losses by persecution the population depended to some extent on replenishment by young birds dispersing from more densely occupied country further west. That this would be less likely to occur in the years immediately following the spread of myxomatosis, because of the lowered output of young in the buzzard's strongholds, is supported by John Ash's figures for the numbers of buzzards occurring on a Hampshire chalkland estate (in an area carrying no breeding buzzards) between 1952 and 1959. Ash showed that there was normally an autumn peak of numbers, presumably due to an influx of young birds from breeding areas, but that this was poorly marked in 1955 and failed to occur at all in 1956. A paucity of buzzard sightings continued, in fact, until autumn 1957.[34]

Of the counties on the eastern fringe of the buzzard's range, only Sussex seems to have retained a substantial resident population throughout the 1950s, though the evidence is inadequate to determine relative breeding success over this period. Certainly at least one pair bred in each of the four years from 1954 to 1957, and several others were known to be present. Although C. G. des Forges and D. D. Harber suggested in 1963 that the buzzard's position in Sussex had 'deteriorated'[35] since myxomatosis, the records in the annual *Sussex Bird Report* suggest rather that this outlying population has remained remarkably stable at around six or eight pairs from about 1964 to the present time, evidently the result of protection—or at least the absence of persecution—in the districts colonised.

In northern England and in Scotland, the decimation of the rabbit seems generally to have had a less marked effect on either the breeding success or populations of buzzards. Population densities comparable to those in south-west England and Wales were only achieved further north before 1954 on some of the smaller offshore islands, and it is to be assumed that in the more spacious conditions of the north the loss of the rabbit did not generate the intensive intraspecific competition which must have played an important part in regulating population densities after myxomatosis further south. In an analysis of the data on breeding buzzards in the Sedbergh area of north-west Yorkshire for the period 1937–67, Michael Holdsworth was unable to show any clear correlation between the decrease in the rabbit population after 1954 and the numbers or breeding success of the buzzards; though unfortunately no records were available for the critical year of 1955 itself. He did, however, demonstrate that breeding success tended to fluctuate more after myxomatosis than before, and was able to relate this to fluctuations in the population of short-tailed voles, which probably formed the most important single prey species of the buzzard after about 1955.[36]

Even in Wales and the South, there were areas in which the indirect impact of myxomatosis on the buzzard was minimal. In Glamorgan, the buzzard population of the Gower peninsula actually rose from fifteen pairs in 1954 to eighteen pairs in 1956, and the author of the county bird history considered that the buzzard also remained unaffected by the disappearance of the rabbit elsewhere in the county.[37] Norman Moore mentioned that in a part of central Wales the buzzard had also remained unaffected, but in that area rabbits had never been very abundant, whereas the Gower cliffs had certainly supported substantial numbers—though Glamorgan as a whole carried only a low population.[38]

In sum, it would appear that the virtual loss of rabbit prey most severely affected the breeding success and population of the buzzard in those areas where very high—one is tempted to call them 'plague'—populations of rabbits had enabled the buzzard, in turn, to achieve high density populations. The effects were less marked where the rabbit was more thinly or irregularly distributed and where, also, the density of breeding buzzards was lower. Norman Moore emphasised that the reduction in breeding activity in 1955 was not necessarily due directly to lack of rabbit prey, but was more likely to be due to a general reduction in prey resulting from the disappearance of the rabbit. He suggested that the loss of the rabbit would have led to the reduction of other small mammal populations, both by buzzards and other predators which would be competing with each other for a progressively diminishing food resource.[39] More recently, Michael Holdsworth has postulated a slightly different situation. He has pointed out that the numbers of nestling kestrels and barn owls ringed in Britain in 1955 was unusually low. Both of these predators are largely dependent on short-tailed voles, and their breeding success is well known to fluctuate with the size of the vole population. On this basis, he suggested that the effects of myxomatosis in 1955 were probably aggravated by a scarcity of the main alternative mammalian prey species to the rabbit and, further, that the recovery of the buzzard population after 1955 might have been associated with that of the vole population.[40] It would probably be unprofitable to pursue this chicken-or-egg situation in the absence of considerably more information than is now likely to emerge.

In most affected areas, readjustment of buzzard populations to relative stability at a lower level than before myxomatosis seems to have been achieved by about 1958 or 1959. A factor of which the significance in reducing the number of buzzards is difficult to evaluate, is that of human predation. There was undoubtedly a considerable increase in the middle and late 1950s, in the numbers of buzzards shot and trapped in south-west England and in Wales (if not elsewhere), because it was widely believed that in the absence of the rabbit, buzzards would transfer their attention to game-birds, poultry and lambs. Norman Moore instanced reports of over four hundred buzzards being shot in three quite small areas in the winter of 1955. For a while there was considerable pressure to legalise the shooting of buzzards, and this gave rise to many protestations by naturalists of the buzzard's innocence. At one stage the national press became interested in the controversy and, with its usual capacity for reporting exaggerated accounts at face value, printed stories of starving buzzards attacking such improbable targets as farm workers on tractors, shepherds, sheepdogs, full-grown ewes, a lorry driver and—inevitably—a small child in a perambulator.

The increase in persecution may help to answer the question: 'What happened to the surplus birds as populations adjusted to lower densities?' It is not improbable that much of the surplus was creamed off by human persecution. The excess birds would otherwise—presumably—have dispersed elsewhere, or died. The dispersal of large numbers of buzzards away from, say, the South-west Peninsula or Wales, might be expected to have resulted in larger numbers further east and, perhaps, even a further extension of the buzzard's breeding range. That this did not occur confirms that the individual birds died. Whether they died from gun, trap, disease or starvation, there can be no ultimate certainty.

A good starting-point for examining the recent history of

buzzard populations is, perhaps, Ian Prestt's report of the enquiry which he conducted for the British Trust for Ornithology into the status of crows and smaller birds of prey in Britain between 1953 and 1963.[41] The survey was based on a questionnaire which sought the opinions of observers about changes in the status and distribution of the buzzard, sparrowhawk, merlin, kestrel, barn owl, tawny owl, carrion crow, magpie and jay. Of 142 questionnaires completed, 109 were for England, 10 for Wales, 19 for Scotland, 1 for the Isle of Man, 2 for Northern Ireland and 1 for Guernsey. Much of Wales and most of the Scottish Highlands were not covered. As Ian Prestt clearly recognised, the answers to a questionnaire requiring mainly opinions, are open to bias towards popular or fashionable explanations of change. He felt, however, that bias was likely to be minimal in view of the experience of the observers to whom the questionnaires were sent.

Predictably, answers to the questionnaire reflected the widespread reductions in the numbers of buzzards which occurred following the appearance of myxomatosis but, in addition, they recorded a number of more recent and relatively sudden declines which began in the late 1950s and became most evident about 1959 or 1960. These were reported in parts of the northern Pennines and north Westmorland; in the Midlands; and in south Dorset, Wiltshire and west Hampshire. The two main causes suggested were contamination by toxic pesticide residues, and increased persecution by gamekeepers. On the other side of the coin, buzzards were reported to be increasing widely in Dumfriesshire, North Wales, Brecon and Glamorgan and, more locally, in Aberdeenshire, Kirkcudbrightshire, south Westmorland, north Lancashire and the West Riding of Yorkshire. These increases were attributed to reduced disturbance and greater tolerance from keepers and landowners.

The reported declines in the Midlands and southern counties are questionable. They do not appear to be supported by contemporary records or comment in the various annual county bird reports, and there is nothing in my own experience of the three southern counties to confirm the reported decline. Certainly there was no decrease in the population of west Hampshire—effectively my New Forest study area—at the time. I completed the questionnaire for the New Forest, and cannot but wonder somewhat apprehensively which of my comments could be open to misinterpretation. There can, however, be no doubt about the reality of the declines reported from the northern Lake District and adjoining areas of the Pennines.

Describing the situation in Lakeland, Derek Ratcliffe remarked that until myxomatosis the buzzard population had not only maintained its numbers but had shown signs of spreading on to lower ground where there had been none in living memory. Over much of Lakeland there was no appreciable decline in the numbers of buzzards immediately after myxomatosis, even though the rabbit was an important item of prey in the area. After 1958, however, there had been a marked decrease on the Crossfell range, and in the Langdale district a similar decline had commenced on the fells, though there buzzards were apparently continuing to spread into wooded country in the south Lakeland foothills and lowlands. During the 1963 breeding season, Ratcliffe visited 13 buzzard territories which had regularly held breeding pairs up until 1960. Five nests with clutches of 2 eggs were found, and 5 new but empty nests. In the remaining 3 territories no nests at all were found, though pairs of buzzards were present. One of the clutches found was addled and deserted. Of the 5 empty nests, 2 may have been robbed but the remaining 3 had almost certainly never contained eggs, though one was still being brooded by a buzzard. One of the nests with eggs had, in 1962, contained a clutch of 3 which were later found to be broken. Ratcliffe remarked that there was no precedent in the Lakeland buzzard population for the failure of such a large number of territory-holding buzzards to lay eggs, and added that he had never before found an addled clutch of buzzard's eggs. He drew a parallel between this evidence for local decline in breeding success and population in Lakeland, and the situation following myxomatosis in some southern counties. The addled clutch and single eggs from 3 of the other nests were removed for organochlorine analysis. Two of the single eggs were found to contain relatively high concentrations of dieldrin and, besides dieldrin, all 5 eggs contained measurable quantities of DDE, lindane (benzine hexachloride) and heptachlor epoxide.

Lakeland buzzards feed extensively on carrion mutton, and the dieldrin, which was then regularly used in sheep-dips, presumably came from the carcases of dead sheep. The heptachlor probably reached the buzzards through avian prey. Ratcliffe concluded that in view of the comparatively high pesticide residues in the buzzard eggs, and in the absence of any other environmental change, the decline in numbers and breeding success of buzzards in Lakeland could reasonably be attributed to organochlorine pesticide contamination.[42]

The buzzard population in the Lakeland fells seems to have remained depressed throughout the 1960s, and in 1970 R. W. Robson wrote that in north Westmorland he was now finding only about a third of the number of nests found ten years previously, in addition to which clutch sizes had tended to become smaller.[43] In the Midlands and the south and south-western counties of England, buzzard numbers and distribution seem to have remained static through the 1960s. In Wales local increases have occurred, though no widespread population trend is discernable. Only in Scotland—and especially in the Highlands, which were scarcely covered by Ian Prestt's survey—has there been a general and sustained increase and eastward spread.

The organochlorines came into widespread use as agricultural pesticides in the 1940s and 1950s. DDT and benzine hexachloride (BHC) were first used, mainly in orchards, soon after World War II, and quickly found a widening range of applications in crop protection. After 1947 they became widely used in sheep-dips as a protection against blow-fly and tick. In the mid-1950s a number of pesticides belonging to the cylcodiene group of chlorinated hydrocarbons—mainly dieldrin, aldrin and heptachlor—came into use, mainly as seed dressings, though dieldrin started to replace DDT in sheep-dips. All these substances are persistent in animal tissues and —necessarily—toxic. By the late 1950s and early 1960s organochlorine insecticides were widely distributed in the ecosystem. DDT residues, for example, were found in fish, adelie penguins, skuas and seals from Ross Island in the Antarctic.[44] In Britain, measurable amounts of pesticide residues have been found, for example, in populations of seabirds,[45] great crested grebes,[46] and herons.[47] In the late 1950s and the early 1960s, cereal seed dressings containing aldrin, dieldrin and heptachlor resulted in large kills among many gramnivorous birds in the English lowlands.[48] The incidence of substantial organochlorine residues in birds of prey in Britain, and the correlation with breeding failure and declining populations, was referred to in Chapter One. The species most dramatically affected were the peregrine, sparrowhawk and golden eagle. All three species exhibited a high incidence of clutch depletion or loss which could often be attributed to the eating or breaking of their eggs by the parent birds, and Derek Ratcliffe showed that this was associated with significant decreases in eggshell weight and thickness.[49] Declines in the breeding success and population of the peregrine and sparrowhawk were general in the 1950s and 1960s.[50] Both species are bird feeders, and were evidently accumulating residues obtained via their grain and insect-eating prey. Reduced breeding success in the golden eagle population of west Scotland between the mid-1950s and about 1965 was associated with contamination by dieldrin, which reached the eagles via the carrion mutton which in sheepwalk districts formed an important food item.[51]

Concern about environmental contamination by pesticides brought a voluntary ban in Britain, in 1962, on the use of dieldrin, aldrin and heptachlor in seed dressings, whilst many other uses of these substances were voluntarily banned two years later—though it should be remembered that a good deal of stockpiling by farmers went on before the bans on distribution came into effect. In 1966 the use of aldrin and dieldrin in sheep-dips was banned—not, it should be added, because of the adverse effects on the eagle population, but because of fears arising from the levels of dieldrin appearing in meat fat. As a result of the decreased amounts of organochlorine pesticides being released into the environment, gradual recoveries in the populations and breeding success of the affected predators have commenced—in itself not the least convincing evidence for the effects of contamination.[52]

Except in districts where sheep carrion is taken, buzzards generally are likely to have remained comparatively free of pesticide residues because they do not specialise in prey species (such as grain-eating birds) which, in turn, are particularly exposed to contamination. Ratcliffe showed that the average level of organochlorine residues found in buzzards' eggs in Britain in the 1950s and 1960s was low compared with most other raptors, although the mean figure for total residues (1·83 parts per million of egg content without shell) was comparable with that in the golden eagle population of west Scotland between 1963 and 1965 (1·80ppm), before the ban on dieldrin sheep-dips started to take effect. He did not, however, detect any significant difference in the weight or thickness of 83 eggshells collected between 1906 and 1945, and 96 collected between 1948 and 1966.[53] Nevertheless, there was clearly individual and local variation in residue levels: the decreased breeding success in Lakeland was associated with levels higher than the average. There are, too, indications that egg-breaking may have been widespread phenomenon in the 1950s and 1960s. Ratcliffe referred to a broken clutch in Lakeland in 1962, and to a clutch of two broken and two addled eggs seen by L. MacNally near Fort Augustus in Inverness-shire in 1964.[54] In an analysis of the nest record cards for the buzzard, completed for the British Trust for Ornithology up to 1969, I found 21 instances in which clutches were recorded as having been broken—8 from my study population in the New Forest between 1964 and 1969; 2 from Somerset in 1950 and 1968; 3 from Lakeland in 1958 and 1959; 4 from Wales in 1950, 1954, 1956 and 1957; 1 from Dumfries in 1954; 1 from Speyside in 1965; 1 from Ross in 1957; and 1 from Sutherland in 1965.[55] To these can be added a further 4 clutches found broken in the New Forest in 1970 and 1971. In at least 17 instances out of the total of 25, the nature of the breakages was consistent with damage by the adult birds as it was described by Ratcliffe for the peregrine—comminuted shell, often held together by the lining membranes, and occasionally complete shells save for a gaping hole.[56] In some instances, in the New Forest at least, the eggshell damage was in my opinion equally consistent with predation by crows, though a crow will normally remove an egg from a nest in order to suck it. At Speyside in 1965, however, the Hon Douglas Weir disturbed a buzzard actually in the act of eating its eggs. In three other cases the nest record card recorded a progressive depletion of the clutch over a number of days—much as Ratcliffe recorded for the peregrine. Fifteen addled eggs collected between 1963 and 1968 in the New Forest contained only very small amounts of organochlorine residues: the mean figure for total residues (1·32ppm of egg content without shell), was lower than that recorded by Ratcliffe in Lakeland (2·5ppm). I understand from Douglas Weir that analyses of eggs from the Speyside buzzard population, which he has been studying since about 1964, have also yielded minimal residues.

Twenty-one broken clutches represented only 3·4 per cent of the total number of nests (625) whose outcome was recorded on the nest record cards between 1948 and 1969. A further 11·5 per cent were lost because the eggs were addled or deserted, because eggs or young disappeared without trace, or because the young died on the nest; and 8·5 per cent of nests failed because of human predation. Ignoring the last category for the moment, the proportion of territory-holding buzzards which failed to rear young was substantial (14·9 per cent), and in fact must have been an even larger proportion of the population than the cards suggest since they were only filled in for nests which contained eggs or young: non-breeding pairs were not recorded, and in some districts at least these were numerous—for example in such biologically different areas as the New Forest between 1961 and 1971; Lakeland in 1963; Speyside in the late 1960s; and Skomer between 1954 and 1964. In the absence of evidence for higher levels of contamination in buzzard populations it would be wrong to claim a firm correlation between the relatively high frequency of non-breeding and breeding failure, and pesticides, particularly since there is inadequate information about the incidence of such occurrences for any period before the 1950s. Egg-breaking in itself is no evidence of pesticide contamination, and is likely to be a normal adaptive response to various adverse conditions such as a sudden decline in the amount of prey available, severe weather or ill-health. In this connection, however, it is interesting that egg-breaking by the parent birds was not reported as a feature of the myxomatosis episode, and it would be unwise to discard the notion that organochlorine contamination had a depressive effect on the breeding success of the buzzard population during the 1950s and 1960s, combining with the continued high level of human predation to place a brake on the further expansion of the buzzard in England and Wales. In Scotland (and especially in the Highlands) buzzards continued to spread eastwards during the 1960s, especially, one is often told, after the banning of dieldrin in sheep-dips, though it is seldom that definite evidence is available to illustrate this point. The Antrim coast was recolonised once again in the middle of the decade, and by 1969 reports were being received of attempted breeding elsewhere in Ulster. With decreasing amounts of organochlorines in the environment, it will be interesting to see what the future holds for the buzzard further south, especially in districts—like Lakeland—where it has suffered a definite decline. As in the past, however, the buzzard's future status is likely to depend mainly on the attitudes of those who preserve game.

Norman Moore showed that in 1954 there remained an adverse relationship between the respective distributions of buzzards and gamekeepers in Britain. His map showing the relative density of gamekeepers is reproduced as Fig 4, and if this is compared with Fig 3, which shows the relative density of buzzard populations in Britain in 1954, it will be seen that buzzards and keepers tended to be mutually exclusive in distribution. The correlation is not absolute, nor would one expect it to be: the information was plotted mainly by counties, which necessarily obscure the finer details of the situation, and it must also be remembered that the attitudes of keepers and landowners vary. The New Forest, for example, is shown as possessing a high density of keepers but, also, a high density of buzzards, but the map naturally fails to convey the information that the buzzards were not persecuted. None the

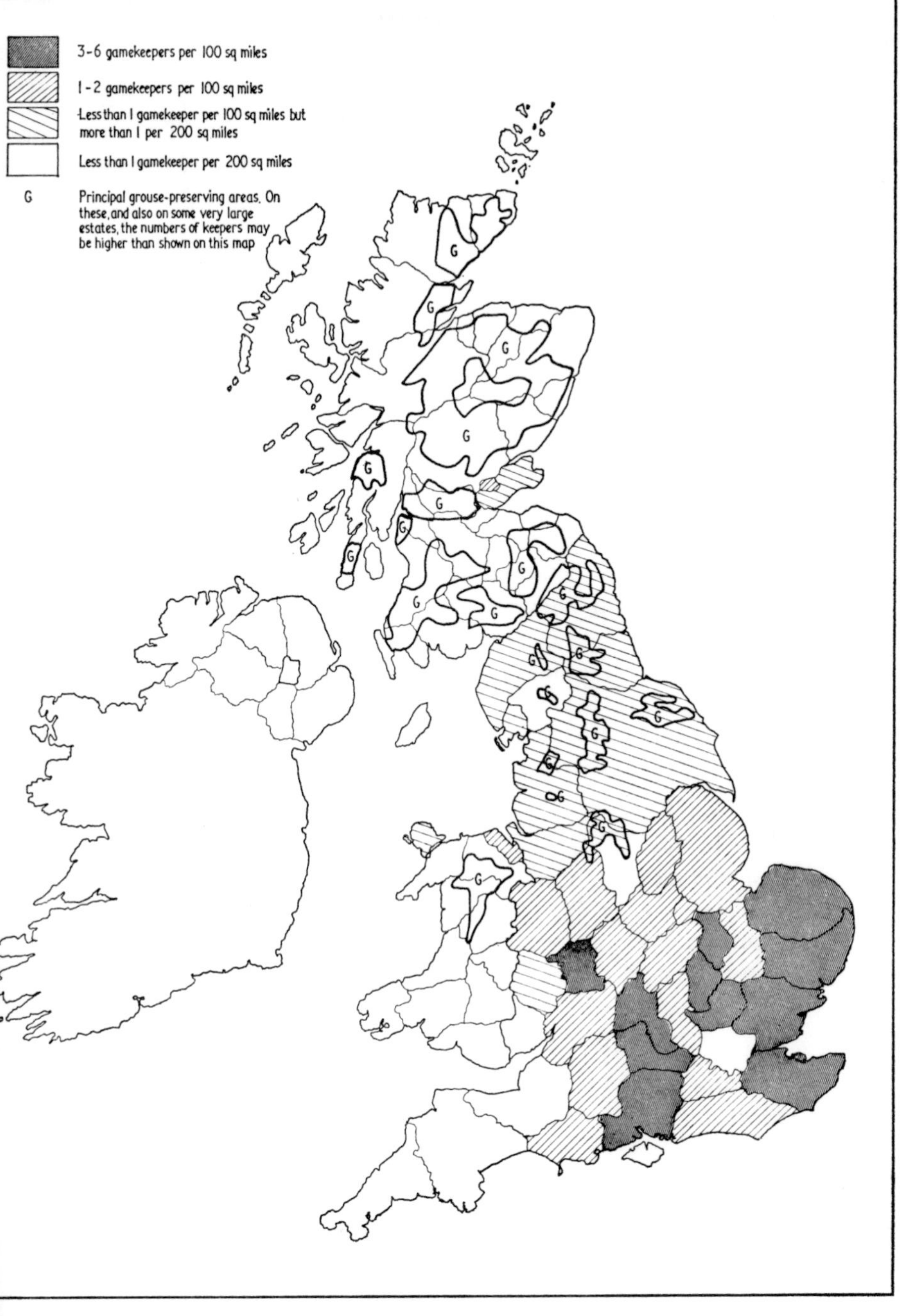

4 Game preservation in the British Isles in 1955 (reproduced from N. W. Moore, *Brit Birds*, 50 (1957), 189)

less, the general conclusion that persecution was the main factor limiting the distribution of the buzzard in 1954 is inescapable.

The distribution of buzzards and gamekeepers in 1972 is not fundamentally different to that in 1954,[57] and the obvious inference is that persecution remains the main factor holding down numbers and limiting the distribution of the buzzard. Indeed, there is a widespread belief among conservationists that the persecution of birds of prey has intensified in very recent years and, indeed, that it may be retarding the recovery of some species which were reduced by pesticides: certainly this view has been propounded by the Director of the Royal Society for the Protection of Birds—a body hardly given to hysterical utterances.[58] The affluent society of the 1960s undoubtedly generated demands for shooting among a widening spectrum of the community. Shooting values of land have escalated, and the shooting syndicate, often comparatively impersonal and detached from close links with the land, has blossomed again. Inevitably, a demand for good, consistent bags exerts pressures on the keeper, one of whose responses is often to intensify the trapping and shooting of predators. In an article written in mid-1971 Derek Barber asserted his belief that this was occurring widely:

> Having pursued some personal researches over two or three years, I am left in no doubt about the extremist policies being followed over significant areas of the Midlands, the Home Counties and parts of Scotland. All in all, it is impossible to escape the conclusion that the modern development of a sizeable shoot presages, more often than not, a less tolerant attitude towards birds of prey.[59]

There are many objective observers who would support this as a fair summary of the situation, though at the same time it would be most unjust not to recognise the tolerance towards predators shown by many landowners and keepers.

Confirmation that persecution of raptors was widespread was provided when, in the spring of 1971, the Royal Society for the Protection of Birds launched a campaign against the illegal killing of raptors and, particularly, against the use of the pole-trap—made illegal in England and Wales as early as 1904, though not until much more recently in Scotland. Not unnaturally there was a certain amount of indignant reaction towards the implied suggestion that keepers were breaking the law, but the Society's contention that persecution was taking place on a substantial scale was clearly supported by the facts that in the first eight months of the campaigns and despite the minimal chances of detecting offences, evidence was found of birds of prey being killed on fifty-eight estates and over ninety pole-traps were found in use.[60]

Facts about the extent to which the buzzard is currently persecuted are understandably difficult to obtain. From my analysis of the British Trust for Ornithology nest record cards, human predation of nests showed an overall decline during the 1950s and 1960s, and indeed by 1959 was negligible.[61] This, however, should occasion no surprise because there would be little likelihood of buzzards being allowed to breed in the first place on estates where they were intensively persecuted. There are, however, strong indications that shooting, trapping and poisoning account for a substantial number of adult birds. Since 1967 I have collected reports of buzzards being shot or trapped in sixteen localities—in none of which buzzards bred—in Sussex, Hampshire, Wiltshire and Dorset. The Royal Society for the Protection of Birds has in recent years received a sufficient number of reports, mainly referring to keepered estates in the west of England and in Wales, to suggest that persecution may well be holding down the population. In 1971 the Society received reports of the alleged killing of a minimum of 70 buzzards on 13 estates. Most were shot or trapped but 2 of 13 buzzards found dead on an estate in Radnor, and 2 found dead near Minehead in Somerset, were found on analysis to contain up to 500ppm of strychnine. There was also a report of buzzards being killed at alpha-chloralose baits, presumably put down for crows, in Herefordshire. In the previous year, reports to the Society included one report of as many as 46 buzzards killed on a single estate in Wales; and in 1968 the even larger total of 81 buzzards were reported killed on an estate in south-west England.

At the very least, these figures must give rise to grave disquiet because they can only represent more or less random examples of persecution.[62] It is sad that the selfish motivations and prejudices of the nineteenth century persist in the minds of many who preserve game. It is a serious matter that the protection extended to the buzzard and other raptors by the Protection of Birds Act 1954 (and subsequent Orders made under the Act) is still systematically and cynically ignored.

Finally, in this chapter it is relevant to ask what, at the end of the day, does the keeper achieve by the slaughter of predators? Certainly all raptors—including the buzzard—take some game-birds and/or their chicks from time to time, and for some species they form an important food source. Golden eagles, for example, feed extensively on red grouse, and the hen harrier in some districts takes large numbers of grouse chicks during the breeding season. It is nevertheless doubtful if even the nineteenth-century slaughter of predators more than marginally increased the bags of game-birds shot. Birds produce numbers of young greatly in excess of those necessary to maintain the adult breeding population. This surplus must be removed between one breeding season and the next by predation, accident, disease or starvation. On a shoot, the surplus population of game-birds provides the sport. The various mortality factors are not additive: two factors operating at the same time do not normally remove more of a population than one factor alone because fundamentally it is the capacity of the environment which ultimately limits the population. There is reasonably convincing evidence that shooting, even on a heavily shot area, will not normally crop the whole of the surplus population and will more often remove less than half of it. It follows, therefore, that the numbers of game-birds taken by predators are unlikely to affect the season's bag of birds shot.[63] Moreover, there is evidence to suggest that predators tend to cream off the ailing, injured or weak, whereas shooting is unlikely to be so selective. There are, indeed, some remarkable accounts in the literature of the apparently deliberate selection of weak or injured prey by raptors. Kai Curry-Lindahl, for example, has given a vivid account of the killing, by a golden eagle, of a reindeer calf with a defective foreleg, selected with obvious deliberation from a herd of about two hundred reindeer, about sixty of which were calves of different sizes.[64] In a more systematic study G. Rudebeck showed that 19 per cent of witnessed kills made by four species of raptor (sparrowhawk, goshawk, peregrine and sea eagle) were of obviously abnormal individuals, and that this was a much higher proportion of abnormal birds in a population than was usual in the wild.[65]

Despite these arguments it must be recognised that there may be circumstances in which predation may significantly affect the number of game-birds available for the guns. This possibly arises when individual raptors repeatedly attack a limited population of game chicks. Some tawny owls, for example, can make locally devastating inroads into the numbers of pheasant poults before the season starts, and buzzards are occasionally guilty of the same heinous crime. Hen harriers sometimes prey almost exclusively on grouse chicks, and where the harrier population is substantial it may conceivably affect the bag later in the year. It must also, incidentally, be remembered that the disturbance caused by eagles, harriers and, more occasionally, buzzards, can badly upset a day's shoot on a grouse moor.

Undoubtedly, there is a need for more research into the relationships between predators and game-bird populations, and the conservationist must be prepared to find that the keeper sometimes has a case. Whether or not it follows that the keeper should be allowed to reduce the numbers of the predator responsible is another matter. It may be necessary to ask if the individual should be allowed to destroy birds (and for that matter mammals) which are part of a heritage common to all.

Chapter Four

SOCIAL BEHAVIOUR

In the absence of human predation the main factors normally regulating buzzard populations would appear to be the availability of prey and nest sites. It would be reasonable to assume that the main mechanism of regulation is the buzzard's own territorial behaviour—in other words that a pair of buzzards will assert and maintain against other buzzards a claim to an area of habitat sufficient to support them and, for part of the year, their young. One of the purposes of my study of the New Forest buzzard population between 1962 and 1971 was to examine the density and distribution of buzzards in relation to the habitat, and to determine the part played by the buzzard's social behaviour in regulating the population. The New Forest is particularly suitable for a study of this kind because the buzzard population there has seen a long period of comparative freedom from human persecution. Egg collectors certainly took their toll earlier in this century, and even today the occasional clutch is stolen; but the interference has for long been minimal compared with most other areas of comparable size. Thus, the buzzard population might be assumed to have achieved stability at a number determined by the capacity of the environment. The factors controlling the population are likely to be more readily apparent than in an area where it is held below capacity by persecution, or where it is still colonising fresh country.

The New Forest lies on the infertile sands and clays deposited in Tertiary times in the downfold of the chalk known as the Hampshire Basin. Geomorphologically it consists today of a series of eroded plateaux, highest in the north, and lowest in the south. In the north, where heights of just over 400ft OD are achieved, stream erosion has left little more than a series of ridges between wide, but comparatively steep-sided valleys. In the south, where the plateaux are mostly at elevations of 50–150ft, they are less fragmented by their drainage systems, and form extensive, undulating plains with shallow valleys and basins in which valley bogs on deep accumulations of peat have developed.

The forest has an individual and complex history, upon which it is worth dwelling briefly. The district emerges into the written record in the eleventh century, when it was appropriated to the Crown as a Royal Forest by William I. A forest in this context had legal connotations unconnected with a woodland cover, and could best be described as an area subject to forest law as distinct from the common law. In the New Forest, as in other English Royal Forests, the early purpose of the Crown was the conservation of deer for hunting and as a source of meat, and to this end the forest law regulated all other activities—and especially the grazing of domestic animals in the unenclosed wastes and woods—which might conflict with deer conservation. In later medieval times the interest of the Crown in the New Forest turned gradually to the enclosure of land for silviculture, which repeatedly provoked conflict with the commoners, who from time immemorial had grazed their animals where the Crown now wished to enclose. From the end of the seventeenth century, successive Acts of Parliament provided for the enclosure of land by the Crown for the growth of timber, and there are today some 20,000 acres of statutory silvicultural enclosures. These occupy a large, central block of the forest, with smaller, outlying areas. Most of the early plantations were of oak, and today, approaching half of the total area remains under deciduous woodland, the remainder carrying a variety of conifer crops, including many stands of Scots pine and Douglas fir of nineteenth-century origin. Some 48,000 acres of the forest remain unenclosed, and legally unenclosable, and subject to the exercise of various rights of common—mainly now those of grazing for ponies and cattle, and of mast. It is of passing interest that the New Forest is probably now the only remaining area in Britain where common of mast—the right to turn out pigs on the mast in the autumn—is still exercised. The respective rights of the Crown, represented since 1925 by the Forestry Commission, as the owner of the soil, and of the commoners, with rights over the soil, are carefully defined in the New Forest Acts 1877–1970, and the land from which the common rights arise is legally registered in an Atlas of Claims to Common Rights.

Today the unenclosed common lands of the New Forest represent the most extensive single tract of unsown or semi-natural vegetation in the lowland zone of Britain—a gently contoured mosaic of beech, oak and holly woodland, heathland, and acid grassland, with valley bogs and fertile alluvial 'lawns' following the drainage pattern. It will be appreciated that this is not a 'primeval' landscape, but one whose character has been shaped from prehistoric times by man and his animals. The heathlands and acid grasslands have arisen as a secondary condition to an early woodland cover, the clearance of the woodland commencing at least by the Middle Bronze Age and continuing into modern times, though checked by the forest law which specifically protected the vert—the woodland—from deliberate exploitation if not from the depredations of the deer and the commoners' animals. Indeed, the large number of deer in the Royal Forest, together with the commoners' cattle and ponies, had profound effects on the regeneration of the unenclosed woodlands, the age structure of which is today closely related to the fluctuations which took place in the numbers of herbivores over the past three centuries or more. The long centuries of grazing have also much modified the species compositions of the woods, for example by eliminating palatable shrubs such as hazel, and by severely impoverishing the ground flora. The commoners' animals have been described as the architects of the forest scenery, and with this the ecologist would scarcely disagree.

It would probably be fair to say that the 8,000 acres of unenclosed woodland in the forest no longer have any strict parallel in Britain. Lowland woods in which man does not terminate the natural life of the trees by felling are extremely rare, and outside the forest persist now only as small fragments. The unenclosed woods of the forest are mainly of beech and oak with an understory of holly. Their edges are irregular and they are interspersed with innumerable clearings and glades. Ecologically they are undoubtedly the finest remnants of relatively undisturbed deciduous woodland in Britain and, probably, in western Europe. Their essential characteristics are an uneven age structure; the widespread representation of mature, senile and decaying trees; and a rich epiphytic lichen and bryophyte flora, and invertebrate, bird, and bat fauna. These characteristics can be directly traced to the relative lack of recent human interference in the sense that though the woods have been casually culled through for timber from time to time, they have not been systematically managed (though most saw some attempt at management in medieval times).[1]

My buzzard study area covered 112 square miles, or roughly 71,500 acres, and included most of the unenclosed common lands and statutory silvicultural enclosures of the forest, together with extensive areas of intermixed and peripheral agricultural and residential land, mostly small-holdings and small farms, mainly in grass, and a number of villages. It contained approximately 32,000 acres of woodland; 33,000 acres of heathland, acid grassland and valley bog; and 6,500 acres of agricultural and residential land. The number of pairs of buzzards present (but not necessarily breeding) in the study area during the ten breeding seasons from 1962 to 1971 varied between 33 and 37. There was, however, some 'turnover' of territories, and a total of 43 were recorded as being occupied at different times during the study period. These are shown conventionally in Fig 5, from which it will be seen that 27 territories were occupied continuously during the study period. The history of the remaining 16 territories between 1962 and 1971 is shown in Fig 6. At least 9 territories unoccupied at the start of the study period, carried pairs of buzzards at the end of it, whilst at least 5 territories occupied in 1962 were abandoned by 1966. One territory was occupied in 1963 and abandoned again in 1969, and another which was occupied in 1962 was abandoned in 1964 but reoccupied in 1969.

Many of the territories recorded on Fig 5, whether occupied

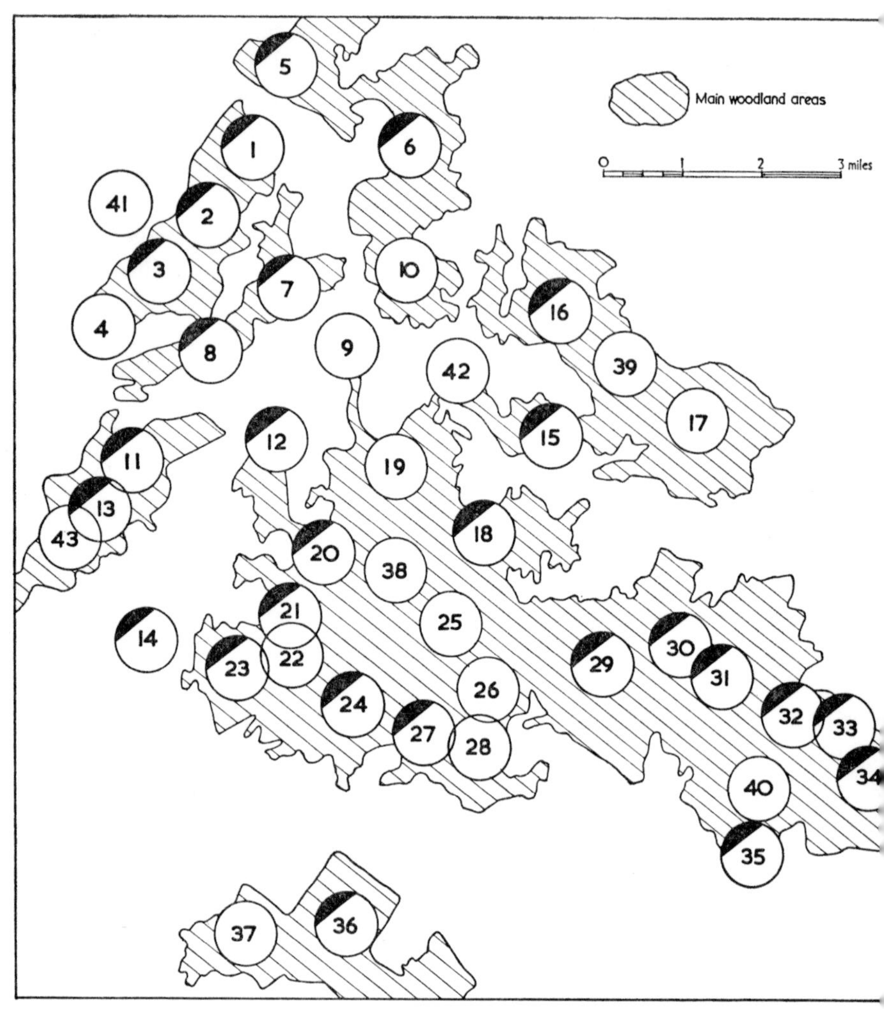

5 Distribution of buzzard territories in the New Forest study area, 1962–71. Territories are shown conventionally by numbered circles of arbitrary size. Part-shaded circles denote territories occupied continuously from 1962–71

continuously between 1962 and 1971 or not, clearly have much older pedigrees, though the record is fragmentary. Of the 27 continuously occupied territories, 9 held pairs from 1928 to 1935 to judge from B. J. Ringrose's records, and at 2 of these, breeding was recorded again in 1943 by P. L. Day. In addition, Day recorded breeding at a further 2 localities continuously occupied during my study period. More recently, within my own experience, 11 territories (including some recorded by Ringrose and Day) held buzzards in each year from 1954 until the start of my study in 1962.

Turning to the 16 territories discontinuously occupied during my study period, of the 9 colonised between 1962 and 1971 at least 3 had been occupied at times in the 1940s and 1950s, and, indeed, 2 of them can be identified in the late nineteenth-century literature. Of the 5 territories abandoned by 1966, 2 held pairs of buzzards

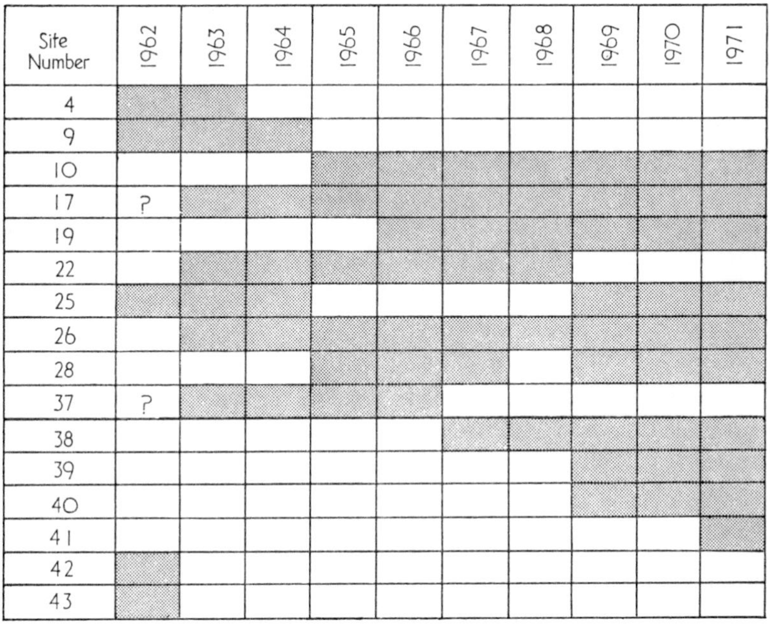

Site Number	1962	1963	1964	1965	1966	1967	1968	1969	1970	1971
4										
9										
10										
17	?									
19										
22										
25										
26										
28										
37	?									
38										
39										
40										
41										
42										
43										

6 History of discontinuously occupied buzzard territories in the New Forest study area, 1962–71. Shading denotes occupation by a pair of buzzards. Site numbers conform with those in Fig 5

between 1928 and 1935, and 2 others were, to my own knowledge, occupied for many years before 1962. The 2 remaining territories were both occupied in 1943 when Day found the nests.

Thus, it would seem that many (perhaps most) of the territories plotted on Fig 5 have long, though not necessarily uninterrupted, histories of occupation by pairs of buzzards. It would be of great interest to know whether some territories are especially prone to periodic abandonment, perhaps because they have some intrinsic disadvantages, or whether abandonment is more a matter of chance. Unfortunately my study period was too short to determine this—one would probably need to know the history of each territory over several decades—but I was certainly unable to distinguish any ecological differences between those territories continuously occupied, and those discontinuously occupied, between 1962 and 1971. The 33–37 pairs of buzzards shared the New Forest study area with large populations of other predatory birds—some 17–20 pairs of kestrels, up to 19 pairs of hobbys, probably around 40 pairs of sparrowhawks, and a large but undetermined number of tawny owls. Each of the first three species sometimes displayed aggression towards buzzards, and it was not uncommon to watch the smaller raptors—and also carrion crows—diving repeatedly at a soaring buzzard, sometimes pressing home their attack hard enough to cause it apparent discomfort, and occasionally provoking it to a display of talons. I found no evidence, however, that aggression by the smaller raptors and crows arose from competition for nest sites (or food), nor did I find any evidence that it affected the occupation of a buzzard territory. Indeed, it was not unusual for buzzards to rear young at less than 200yd from successful nests of the smaller species, though crows sometimes succeeded in taking their eggs. Ravens and peregrines—which compete with the buzzard for nest sites in parts of upland Britain—are regrettably absent from the New Forest as breeding species.

Population densities of raptors tend to be calculated simply by dividing the number of pairs present into the area of the district studied. Certainly this gives one measure of the carrying capacity of the ground, but because the district will almost inevitably have arbitrary boundaries, it will generally include areas which either hold no birds or are hunted over irregularly, and thus the calculation will not necessarily show how much space each pair of birds uses. The New Forest buzzard study area is 112 square miles, and the number of pairs of buzzards present between 1962 and 1971 was 33–37, giving a density of one pair per 3·0–3·3 square miles. Fig 6 shows, however, that although in some parts of the forest the territories were distributed with remarkable regularity, there were extensive tracts which did not contain any, though most of these were hunted by buzzards with varying regularity.

Defended territories were smaller than 3·0–3·3 square miles, and a measure of their average size may be obtained by determining the average distance between nests. For this purpose all nests known to have been occupied during the study period were plotted on large-scale maps, and a measurement made between each nest and its nearest neighbour occupied in the same year. Most territories contained a number of nests in a fairly close group, and for the purpose of measurement each group was treated as a single nest. Isolated nests at a distance from the group were treated separately, so that for some territories two or three measurements were made, each to the nearest neighbouring nest occupied in the same year. The results, given in Table 2, are significantly different from random. Of 54 nests or groups of nests, 40 were between 0·8 and 1·2 miles from their nearest neighbour. The mean distance between all nests or groups of nests was a little under a mile. The few nests lying at greater distances than 1·2 miles from their nearest neighbour were situated in comparatively isolated woodlands. Of those nests less than 0·6 miles apart, 4 were occupied in one year only, and included the remarkable occurrence for the New Forest of 2 nests only about 300yd apart, at territories 21 and 22 in 1962. Spacings of this order are less unusual in parts of Wales and the South-west Peninsula, where population densities of buzzards exceed those in the New Forest. Indeed, I have known of examples in which two and sometimes three buzzard nests have been situated in the same small valley-side wood, only about 300yd in length.

TABLE 2

Distances separating buzzard nests in the New Forest study area 1962–71

Distance (miles)	0·2	0·3	0·4	0·5	0·6	0·7	0·8	0·9	1·0	1·1	1·2	1·3	1·4	1·5
Number of nests	2	—	—	2	4	—	6	15	8	6	5	2	—	4
									mean: 0·95 miles					

Clearly there is a definite spacing mechanism involved in the distribution of buzzard nests. Assuming each territory to be a circle with a radius of half the average distance between nests, the average territory size would be about 0·7 square miles. In practice, of course, most territories partially abut on to areas not occupied by other buzzards, so that they tend to be somewhat larger than 0·7 square miles. Territories actually plotted by observation of buzzard behaviour, however, were seldom more than about 1 square mile in area and were more often between about 0·7 and 1·0 square miles. That the observed territory size is not greatly different from the calculated size is a reassuring check on the validity of the method of calculation, though clearly this is likely to be less useful in areas where buzzard populations are kept well below environmental capacity by persecution.

Assuming 0·7–1·0 square miles per pair of buzzards, the New Forest study area would have a theoretical capacity of well over 100 pairs, whereas during the study period, and probably for many years previously, the population remained relatively static at less than half that number. It is therefore necessary to ask if the study area is occupied below its capacity; whether much of it is unsuitable for buzzard territories; or, a third alternative, whether the 'empty' areas contribute in some essential way to the support of the existing population.

The distribution of buzzard territories in the New Forest is closely related to that of the woodlands. The areas vacant of territories on Fig 5 are mainly open heathlands, grasslands, bogs and agricultural land. The woodland areas offer both nest sites and a diversity of vertebrate prey in the buzzards' breeding season. The large tracts of heathland in the New Forest offer few nest sites and are, faunistically, comparatively impoverished: in particular, they do not support the small rodent populations found, for example, on sheepwalks in upland Britain. Nevertheless, it is perhaps surprising that few buzzard territories in the New Forest include much agricultural land, because the small grass fields, abundant hedgerows and pieces of 'waste' ground are a habitat which, in the South-west Peninsula, is well populated with buzzards.

Most territories in the New Forest consist mainly of woodland and woodland-edge habitats, and most of the prey is sought for within them; but most pairs of buzzards also hunt over a considerably larger area than that to which they assert a claim by aggression towards intruders. Almost all the vacant areas of the forest were hunted by buzzards during my study period, particularly when the adults were feeding young in the nest, and again in the winter and early spring when the hedgerows and small fields of the patches of agricultural land in and around the forest probably offered more prey than the woodlands. Individual buzzards or pairs of buzzards often developed regular feeding grounds well beyond the confines of the defended territory—sometimes up to two or three miles away—and in a sense these might be regarded as extensions of the territory, except that few attempts were seen to defend them against intruders. It is probable, however, that the territory can only be regarded as the nucleus of the space required by a pair of buzzards, and that it functions as a basic reservoir of food normally supplemented by hunting a more extensive area. In this context 3·0–3·3 square miles per pair of buzzards probably represents roughly the area hunted by most New Forest pairs.

Despite what has been said, it would nevertheless seem that during the 1962–71 study period the New Forest held somewhat fewer pairs of buzzards than it was capable of supporting. This is suggested by the 'turnover' of territories during the study period alone. There seems no reason why most of the forty-three territories shown on Fig 5 should not have been simultaneously occupied, for most have shown that they can support buzzards, not just temporarily but for a number of years. Territories with discontinuous occupation histories may, as suggested earlier, possess some intrinsic disadvantage, but if there was substantial recruitment of young birds to the adult breeding population, one would expect them to remain occupied. In some cases—for example site 4, abandoned in 1964, and site 9, abandoned in 1965—observation showed that the vacant territories were only hunted occasionally by nearby pairs of buzzards after the disappearance of their occupants. Both territories had a long history of continuous occupation before the start of my study period. None of these facts supports the hypothesis that competition was responsible for squeezing the territory out of existence. There are, too, a few blocks of woodland which did not carry buzzards at all during my study period, and which would appear to represent genuinely 'vacant' spaces, rarely hunted by established pairs of buzzards and exhibiting no obvious ecological differences to long-occupied territories. In sum, it would appear unlikely that the New Forest study area is 'full', though it is probably not far below the capacity set by the buzzards' territorial behaviour, which in turn is likely to be a mechanism for regulating the population in relation to the available prey-biomass.

How does the population density and territory size of the New Forest buzzard population compare with elsewhere? The maximum density recorded in Britain was the 7·08 pairs/square mile on Skomer Island in 1954, referred to in Chapter One. In Norman Moore's 1954 survey, densities of 3·87 pairs/square mile were recorded from Monmouth; 2·6 and 2·3 pairs/square mile from Devon; and 2·5 pairs/square mile from Argyll. All these densities, however, appear to have been exceptional, and probably depended on massive rabbit populations. I would concur with Moore's suggestion that 1–2 pairs/square mile would be a more normal maximum density in a favourable habitat. In a Carmarthenshire valley in July 1964, I found 12 pairs feeding broods in an area of 8 square miles—a density of 1·5 pairs/square mile, which was probably below true density because no account was taken of unsuccessful breeding pairs. There are other examples of comparable densities from Wales and south-west England. Peter Dare, who studied a population of buzzards on the edge of Dartmoor over the period 1956–8, recorded a density of 1–1·2 pairs/square mile. His study area, like the Carmarthenshire valley, embraced a wide range of habitats—nearly 13 square miles of farmland, small deciduous woods, young conifer plantations, open moor and heathy common—and offered a diversity of prey.[2] On the open Lakeland fells in the Sedbergh area, on the other hand, Michael Holdsworth recorded the much lower density of 1 pair to 3·4 square miles, which he also equated with territory size—little different to the New Forest.[3] The Hon Douglas Weir, studying the buzzard population of Speyside, an area which is still being colonised (or more correctly, recolonised) by the species, recorded an intermediate density of about 1 pair to 1·8 square miles in 1970—33 pairs on about 60 square miles.

On the Continent of Europe the buzzard seldom appears to achieve densities as high as those in the most favourable British habitat. In the Berlin area between 1940 and 1951, for example, Wendland found an average density of about a pair to 1·7 square miles; and in four study areas in north-west Germany, Warncke and Wittenberg recorded densities ranging between 0·7 and 3·2 square miles per pair.[4]

The low population density of buzzards in the New Forest, where they have gone unmolested by man for many years, is likely to reflect a low density of readily available prey, especially rodent populations. Small clutch sizes appear to be a further adaption to this situation, which is discussed further in Chapter Six. One would perhaps expect a comparatively low prey-biomass to be further associated with large territories. Apart from my New Forest study, the only British work which has included calculations of territory size and studies of territorial behaviour would seem to be that of Peter Dare on Dartmoor during 1956–8, and the Hon Douglas Weir and Nick Picozzi in Speyside from 1969 to the time of writing. Dare's population—12 pairs in 1956 and 14 pairs in 1957 and 1958—defended territories varying from 130 to 580 acres in size and averaging 350 acres. The territories occupied rather less than half the study area, but as in the New Forest the birds ranged well beyond their territory boundaries in their quest for food. In Speyside, territories of established pairs were of the order of 500 acres. In the New Forest they ranged in size from 320 to 684 acres and averaged 460 acres. They were thus larger than those on the edge of Dartmoor but little different from those in Speyside. In Germany, M. Melde recorded breeding territories of the order of 250 acres,[5] and in the well wooded country of Lorraine, Jean-Marc Thiollay recorded even smaller territories of 80–240 acres.[6] In both continental studies the territories formed only part of the complete hunting range of the buzzards. Clearly, much more comparative data is necessary before firm conclusions can be drawn, but what is perhaps remarkable is that there is so little difference in territory size between such widely divergent habitats as Speyside, where rabbits were abundant and broods were large, and the New Forest, where rodents were few and broods were small. It is equally surprising that continental buzzards, which depend heavily on voles, tend to occupy smaller territories than those in a British study area rich in rabbits.

From what has been said, it seems that the density and distribution of buzzards are largely regulated in the New Forest study area by the buzzards' own territorial behaviour, and by the distribution of woodland and part-woodland areas where the greatest diversity of prey is available and where tree nest sites are available. In this and the following sections it is intended to focus more closely on the territorial behaviour of the buzzard, drawing mainly on my observations in the New Forest. That the vigorous territorial behaviour of the buzzard is no local phenomenon is confirmed by Peter Dare's observations on the edge of Dartmoor, and by the Hon Douglas Weir's more recent observations in Speyside; and, indeed, it will be evident to any careful observer watching buzzards wherever they are reasonably numerous.

The buzzard is a good species for the study of territorial behaviour because territories are comparatively small and can often be overlooked by the human observer from a single vantage point, and because much of the buzzard's assertive behaviour takes place conspicuously in the air over the territory.

The prolonged soaring of buzzards may to the casual observer appear functionless or, if given a human parallel, a kind of leisure activity. The group of three or four buzzards in the air together, tumbling, and chasing each other may be interpreted as sheer *joie de vivre*. In fact the buzzard's soaring behaviour functions largely as a means of territorial advertisement, and the tumbling and chasing is likely to represent a territorial dispute occasioned by the intrusion of one pair of soaring birds over the territory of another. Soaring also, of course, serves as a means of locating prey over large areas with the minimum of effort.

Buzzards maintain territories throughout the year, but territorial activity appears most intensive in early spring—from as early as mid-January if the weather is mild and conditions permit soaring—prior to incubation, and again in July and early August when the adults are feeding large young. There is another definite phase of intensive territorial activity again in the late autumn, after the young have dispersed, which presumably marks the assertion of winter territories. All three periods, and especially the first, are marked not only by aggression between individual buzzards and pairs of buzzards from different territories, but also by courtship display flights. Even in spring these appear to me to function as much as an assertion of territory as a courtship flight. Normally they take three forms. The simplest consists of the pair soaring round each other in tight circles directly over the territory, facing each other, the male normally but not invariably above the female, and sometimes diving down at her. This is often accompanied by repeated, ringing 'Ca . . . ow' calls—how the buzzard's call can ever be described, as it so often is, as a plaintive mew I have never understood—and frequently (usually in March and April when nest building or repairing is in progress) the male will carry a small branch in his talons—indeed I have sometimes watched a bird soaring with what could be better described as a small bough, green with foliage, in his talons, though presumably it could have been of no great weight. More occasionally the branch will be replaced by prey. This simple soaring flight frequently leads into the more complicated diving display flight in which the male sweeps up into the wind with a few wing flaps and a fast glide, stalls, tips forward and plunges earthward on closed or semi-closed wings for a hundred, perhaps even two hundred feet, before pulling out of the dive by spreading its wings (the strain on the wing muscles at this point must be terrific) and then shooting upwards again, the body becoming practically vertical at the top of the ascent immediately before the bird stalls again, tilts over and plunges down once more. These dives may be repeated a dozen times or more—twenty successive undulations are not uncommon—the bird generally working in a rough circle over the territory—though sometimes wandering well beyond it and in doing so incurring the attentions of another territory holder—the dives becoming shallower and shallower until they are little more than a series of undulations, reminiscent of a green woodpecker's flight. As the dives become shallower, so more of both the downward and upward movements take place on more or less spread wings. Extraordinarily enough this diving display is sometimes performed with a small branch or prey still held in the talons. At times, two or more pairs from adjoining territories may be displaying simultaneously (and often, apparently, 'against' each other), and on these occasions the air can seem full of buzzards, the males 'bouncing' across the sky like slow-motion rubber balls, the females often drifting together, an intruder over another's territory provoking much calling and eventually an aerial chase. Occasionally the female of a pair will perform the diving display, and it is sometimes difficult to decide whether two displaying birds are males from different territories or a pair from the same territory—or even, conceivably, females from adjoining territories. The male buzzard is slighter, somewhat narrower winged, than the female, but these distinctions are not always obvious, and even after years of watching buzzards it is often difficult to distinguish the sexes.

There is a third, and quite different, form of display flight which I have watched frequently enough in the New Forest but seldom elsewhere. In this, the soaring bird, usually comparatively low over the territory, breaks into a level flight in which the wings are raised high above the body and pass very deliberately downwards to a point well below the body. The bird usually progresses in an arc, the long wing strokes and deceptively slow movement leaving an almost owl-like impression—short-eared owls have a display flight which is not dissimilar. I have never watched this display flight performed by the female, and on most occasions she has remained soaring. On a number of occasions, however, I have watched it performed by the male alone (though the female may have been below him among the crowns of the trees), and then it seemed almost as though he was patrolling the territory rather than performing a courtship flight. Indeed, this flight may function as a posture of aggression towards intruders, for on two occasions—once in the New Forest and once in Carmarthen—I watched it terminate in a sudden dash downwards in pursuit of another buzzard which must have been hunting, or perhaps merely sitting about, in the patrolling bird's territory, the two birds, pursuer and pursued, twisting off low among the trees before going up into a soar, the intruder finally drifting away from the area. I have found only one published reference to this display flight and that is in the *Handbook of British Birds* (1943 edn) where F. C. R. Jourdain and B. W. Tucker mentioned that a 'flight display with long sweeping wing strokes like displaying Goshawk has been once recorded on Continent'. It is, indeed, a very accipiter-like display, and it is tempting to draw attention to the fact that in the New Forest the buzzard, like the accipiters, is essentially a woodland bird.

Coition, on the comparatively few occasions on which I have witnessed it, has taken place on one of the regularly used perches—often a boundary marker tree—in the territory, the female soliciting the male with movements of the wings and tail. It has never followed immediately on a display flight, which tends, perhaps, to lend weight to the suggestion that display may be associated largely with the assertion of territory.

Although often very difficult to draw on a map, each buzzard territory has definite boundaries, the violation of which provokes an aggressive reaction from the occupants. Such incidents are often prolonged, and often take the participants some distance from the source of dispute. The appearance of a buzzard or pair of buzzards over another pair's territory, once detected, invariably tempts one or both of the occupying pair into the air, calling, spiralling up to challenge the intruders. Often enough, little happens. The birds circle together in the same thermal for some while, and eventually the intruders glide off, unmolested. On other occasions the occupier of the territory will stoop at one of the intruders and the two will go twisting and turning, sometimes literally cartwheeling downwards, occasionally with talons actually locked together, breaking away to swoop up and gain height again before the chase continues, the whole incident punctuated with wild 'Ca . . . ow' calls, the pitch and length depending on the emotional state of the birds, or, to suggest a different interpretation, on the excitement of the moment. The cartwheeling downward plunge of the two birds with interlocked talons has also been interpreted as a form of display in some other large raptors, the participants being the male and female of a pair; but I have to admit that on the occasions on which I have seen it in the buzzard I have attributed it to a dispute between two males.

It is often possible to detect a buzzard intruding over another's territory without, at first, seeing either of the birds: a long, wild, wavering 'Ca . . . aow . . .' from the crowns of the trees will herald the appearance of a buzzard rising to greet the intruder, and often it is not until one has followed the bird soaring into the sky that, finally, the intruding bird or birds suddenly become visible, high overhead. On other occasions, the challenging calls come out of a clear blue sky in which one seeks the birds in vain, although it is clear that a territory dispute is in progress: eventually, of course, one picks them out, tumbling and chasing across the sky. Under these circumstances it is difficult to ascribe a particular call to a particular bird—certainly both pursued and pursuer call—but I have often been satisfied that the calls which sound more aggressive, more challenging, to the human ear, are indeed those of the occupant of the territory. By the same token it is often, of course, difficult to be sure, after the initial chase, whether the roles of pursuer and pursued remain constant in any one incident. Events are rapid and often confused, especially if three or four birds are involved.

Nevertheless, on all those occasions in which I have been sure of the matter, the occupants of the territory have remained the consistent aggressors until well clear of the territory boundary, even though by that time the birds may be over the intruders' territory. They may equally, of course, drift over yet a third territory, the occupiers of which may in turn join the mêlée. Sometimes as many as six or even eight birds may be soaring and chasing and tumbling in the same thermal, especially in the early spring, and it is then practically impossible to sort out which individuals belong to which territory unless some have distinguishing plumage characteristics—and in the New Forest that is not frequent.

Territorial advertisement is not confined to soaring. Buzzards often have on the boundary of their territory a number of perches to which they return repeatedly, and which appear to me to serve as boundary markers. At some territories I have also recorded what appear to be habitual patrolling flights between these markers, particularly in the early morning and evening when, however, they may equally be interpreted as hunting flights—on three occasions in the New Forest I witnessed the pursuit of birds among the crowns of the trees between markers. Both boundary marker trees and patrolling flights seemed to me to occur most often where two territories adjoined each other, though regular perching on apparent boundary marker trees would also occur where the territory abutted on to a large 'vacant' area of heathland or farmland. Where two territories adjoined, it would not be uncommon to witness the males, or sometimes females, of both pairs pitched in trees not a hundred yards apart, calling repeatedly, the calls rising suddenly in pitch as one of the birds left its marker tree and chased through the trees after the other. Territorial boundary disputes of this kind were particularly valuable in plotting territories.

Buzzard territories clearly have a vertical as well as a horizontal dimension, though the former is not easy to determine. Aggressive territorial behaviour, however, appears to be concentrated below a height which may vary in different areas between 400 and 800ft. In hill country it is comparatively easy to decide the maximum height above which territorial behaviour ceases, because it is possible to measure the altitude of soaring buzzards against hills of known height. My impression in the valleys of south-central Wales in 1965 and 1966, for example, was that territories extended vertically to about 800ft from the valley floor. In the New Forest—a gentler landscape—such estimation is more difficult, but my impression has been that around 500ft usually marks the approximate vertical dimension of territories, though territorial disputes sometimes continue above this height if they began below it. It is usually above the vertical limits of territories that the communal soaring of numbers of buzzards occurs. These buzzard 'circuses' begin often enough with buzzards from one territory 'seeing off' those from another, the birds soaring higher and higher in a favourable thermal and gradually drifting together with birds from other thermals until as many as a dozen may be spiralling together in what is presumably a form of communal display, the purpose of which is not clear: or perhaps, like Gilbert White's honey buzzards, they are merely 'inhaling the vapours of the upper air'. Certainly the heights achieved by a buzzard circus—or indeed by pairs of buzzards soaring alone—appear prodigious to the observer on the ground. On many occasions I have lost the birds, still rising, as small dots in the circle of the glasses. Just as extraordinary is the speed with which they can descend, dropping like stones on closed wing, in a series of vertical stoops, pulling out briefly between each one before dropping again, the final stoop often enough taking them into the woodland canopy near the nest.

My observations of buzzards in the New Forest suggest that, as a general rule, the male of a pair is responsible for the advertisement of the territory by boundary perching and the associated boundary flights, though both sexes, singly—when it is normally the male—or together, carry out advertisement soaring over the territory. A further generalisation is that in territorial disputes buzzards usually react to other buzzards of similar sex. This is not invariable, and I have witnessed incidents in which a female buzzard responded to an intruding male over her territory and, less often, the reverse. Nevertheless it is usual for male to react to male, and female to female—a useful rule to remember when plotting territories because it minimises the chances of confusing a pair with two individuals of different sexes from different territories.

The plotting of territories is time-consuming and demands patience, but it is central to any study of the buzzard's social behaviour. In the New Forest it depended mainly on repeated and prolonged observation, often six or seven hours at a stretch, from hillsides and other vantage points overlooking groups of territories, mainly between March and August. The general location of territories is usually evident from the persistence with which their occupiers soar over them. The amount of soaring activity depends on the weather. Ideal conditions are a fine breezy day with well developed cumulus cloud and the associated thermals which enable the birds to keep aloft with the minimum of effort. On any such day, between mid-morning and mid-afternoon—the 'soaring period'—it is relatively easy to locate most of the occupied territories in a given area, especially early in the breeding season, before incubation has commenced. The plotting of territory boundaries is more difficult. My method in the New Forest was to plot on a map each point where a territory boundary was registered by the behaviour of the birds. This sounds simple enough, but in practice boundaries registered by aerial disputes are often difficult to interpret in terms of features on the ground which can be identified on a map. This is especially so in tracts of continuous woodland beneath which distinctive physical features tend to be obscured. An element of subjective judgement in defining territory boundaries was thus inevitable. I found that this could be reduced by observation within a territory in the early mornings and again in the evenings, when most hunting takes place and when the confrontations between buzzards tended to occur at or below the tree canopy. Each such sighting, and indeed each sighting of single buzzards at these times, was valuable in determining more accurately the boundary of a territory roughly plotted by observation from a vantage point—though I spent many more mornings and evenings without even seeing or hearing a buzzard than the reverse.

My original intention was to attempt to plot all the occupied territories in the study area in each of a number of consecutive years. This, however, proved to demand more time than was available. During the breeding seasons of 1963, 1964 and 1965, however, a good picture was obtained of two widely separated groups of territories occupied by a maximum of fifteen pairs in 1963, and a rough check on these groups was maintained during the subsequent years of the study period. Much supplementary information about the buzzard's territorial behaviour was obtained from observation elsewhere in the study area.

The two groups of territories in each of the years 1963, 1964 and 1965 are shown in Figs 7 and 8. Two features are immediately apparent: first, the relationship between buzzard territories and woodland, remarked upon earlier in the chapter; and secondly the stability of territory boundaries from year to year. Though not plotted systematically after 1965, neither group of territories saw any significant boundary changes in the succeeding years of the study period. The only change in the number of occupied territories in either group after 1965, was the appearance in 1971 of an additional pair which occupied a 'vacant' area of woodland among the group of territories shown on Fig 8. This did not result in any discernible modification in the boundaries of adjoining territories. Not only were the same territory boundaries defended in successive years, but the same boundary marker trees remained in use. These usually occupied commanding positions near, but not necessarily on the edge of, the territories. Sometimes the marker trees of two adjoining territories would be separated by less than 100yd, and in such instances it was not an uncommon sight to see both occupied by male buzzards calling repeatedly at each other. All regularly used marker trees recorded in 1963–5 are shown on Figs 7 and 8, and some of these were still being used in 1971: this is true of at least four marker trees in the group of territories shown in Fig 7, and at least one in the group shown in Fig 8.

Figs 7 and 8 support the hypothesis introduced earlier in this chapter that if the distribution of occupied territories over the available woodland is taken as a criterion, the forest is not occupied to capacity by buzzards. Fig 7, for example, shows a large area of woodland 'vacant' in 1963 and 1964, though it was clearly suitable as a buzzard territory because it was occupied during the 1965 breeding season and, indeed, remained occupied throughout the remainder of the study period. No obvious ecological changes occurred in 1964 which might have made the area attractive as a buzzard territory. Another territory, occupied in the breeding season of 1963, but abandoned during the following winter, was only partly appropriated to an adjoining territory in the spring of 1964. In a third territory, which held a pair of buzzards in the 1963 and 1964 breeding seasons, a single bird was seen once in 1965 and was identified by plumage as the female of the previous season's pair. She was probably not present after the end of June 1965, however, and the territory has remained vacant, and indeed, only occasionally hunted over by buzzards from other territories, ever since. Fig 8 shows considerable areas of woodland unoccupied by buzzard territories in 1963–5, the occupied territories exhibiting a 'cramped' and more or less linear distribution, which it is tempting to interpret as the chance relict of a formerly much larger, dense group of buzzard territories.

Taking 1964 as a sample year, the group of breeding territories shown in Fig 7 varied in size from 540 to 684 acres, and the group in Fig 8 from 360 to 504 acres. The mean territory size in the two groups was 603 acres and 404 acres respectively. There were thus significant differences in territory size between the two groups, and, though it would seem reasonable to assume that this was related to differences in the abundance of prey, no data were available to confirm this. Of the forty-three different breeding territories occupied in the New Forest between 1962 and 1971, thirty-four were measured in one or more years. All fell within the range 320–684 acres, so the groups in Figs 7 and 8 span virtually the whole range of territory sizes recorded in the forest. The mean territory size was 460 acres.

Figs 7 and 8 indicate by means of arrows the approximate directions in which buzzards were most often seen hunting outside the defended territories in the breeding season. The hunting range of a pair of buzzards was certainly several times the size of their territory, and the areas hunted by two or more different pairs of

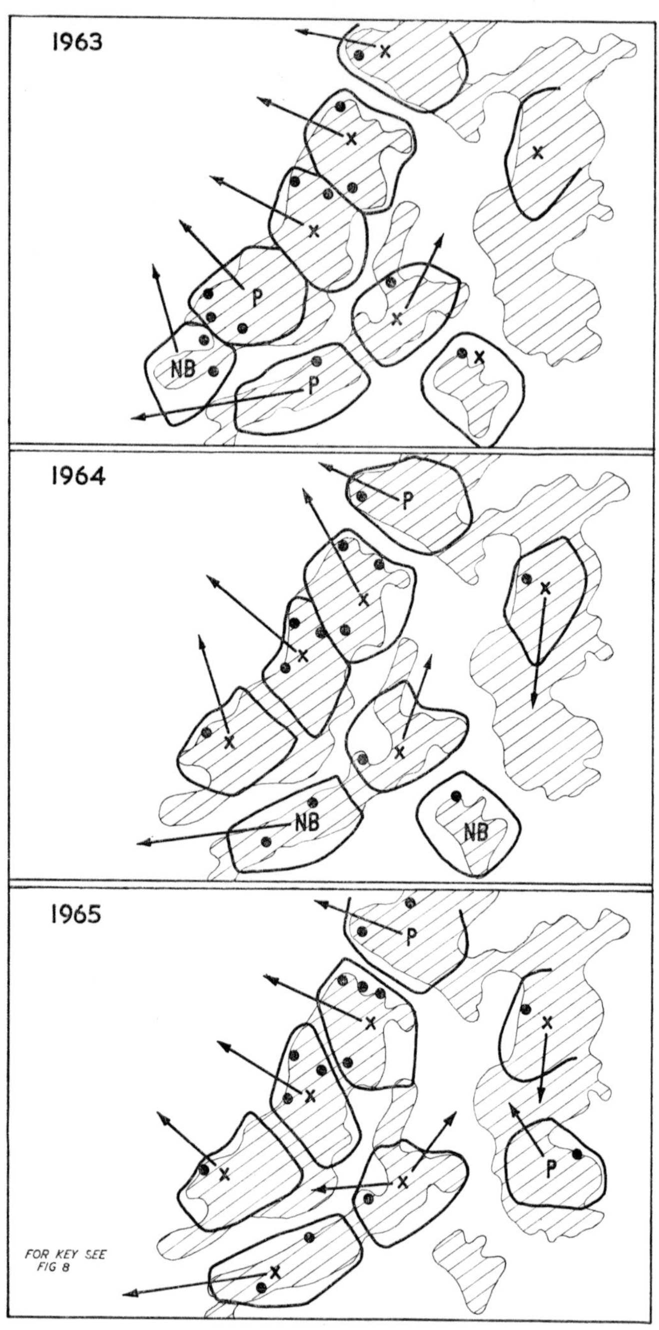

7 Buzzard territories in the New Forest, 1963–5

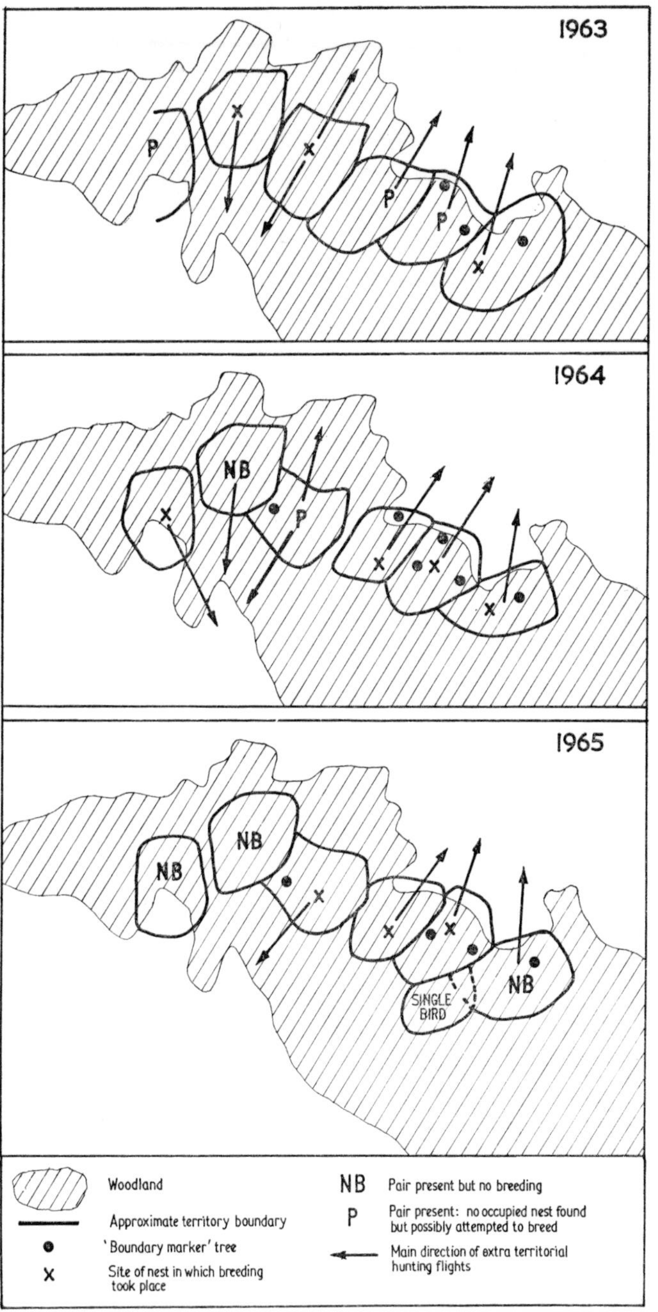

8 Buzzard territories in the New Forest, 1963–5

buzzards frequently overlapped extensively. During the breeding season the exploitation of food sources outside the territory was confined mainly to periods when the weather was suitable for soaring, because the usual method of leaving on an extra-territorial hunting foray was to soar high over the territory and leave in a series of glides from thermal to thermal. This extra-territorial hunting thus tended to take place on fine days between mid-morning and late afternoon. Early morning and evening hunting tended to be confined to the territory or its immediate vicinity. Long hunting flights away from the territory, usually to exploit a rich food source such as a well populated rabbit warren, were most frequently observed during the later stages of the fledgling period, and at these times the distances travelled were often considerable and sometimes took a bird over the territory of another pair—with predictable results.

Not all territory-holding buzzards necessarily bred or attempted to breed each year, but non-breeding pairs (or pairs which lost their eggs early in the season) defended territories as assiduously as successful breeding pairs, and indeed it was often noticeable that non-breeding pairs spent more time soaring over the territory in advertisement—presumably because they had more 'spare' time. This situation is in contrast with Dare's Dartmoor population, in which unsuccessful breeding adults dispersed from the area, usually before July, after which their territory would remain unoccupied until the autumn or later, when an adult pair would again move in. Perhaps as many as 25 per cent of the number of territory-holding pairs of buzzards in the New Forest study area failed to breed in any one year, though it is notoriously difficult to establish failure to breed, and this figure must be regarded as tentative (see Chapter Six). In addition to territory-holding pairs, a small number of single birds could usually be found in the study area during the breeding season. These, too, established definite territories and defended them against intruding buzzards. Their territories, however, were usually smaller than those of established pairs, and the occupants were less inclined to hunt beyond the confines of the territory. The group of territories in Fig 8 included, in 1965, the territory of a

Page 117 (*right*) Clutches of 2–3 eggs are usual (see Table 5); (*below*) adult buzzard incubating

Page 118 (*above*) Adults at nest containing downy young. Voles and other small mammals are brought to the nest in the bill; (*below*) whilst the young remain in down the female rarely moves far from the nest

single bird. This was about 250 acres in area and actually overlapped that of a non-breeding pair. This was large for a territory held by a non-breeding single bird. Six other such territories measured between 1963 and 1967 varied from about 120 acres to 180 acres. It is curious that the single bird should not have taken up a territory in the extensive 'no-man's land' nearby, but I have a second similar record from elsewhere in the forest in which a non-breeding bird occupied a territory overlapping that of a pair which successfully reared two young. Most single birds do, indeed, take up a territory in no-man's land. The number recorded in the study area in the breeding seasons from 1962–71 never exceeded four, though others may have been missed for they were difficult to distinguish among the established pairs unless they possessed distinctive plumage characteristics. In the absence of ringing data (especially colour-ringing) there was no means of determining the origin of these non-breeding birds, or whether they were eventually absorbed into the established territory-holding population, but I was never able to trace one after the end of the year and in no two consecutive years did I record the same 'single' territory occupied.

In the New Forest study area, adult buzzards maintained their territories throughout the year. In winters 1964–5 and 1966–7, during which the buzzard population was under continual observation, I found respectively, 31 out of 33, and 32 out of 33 of the previous breeding season's territories occupied throughout the winter, though it was not always certain that two birds were continuously present: one would, however, expect some individuals to die between one breeding season and the next.

As in spring and summer, the winter population of the study area included a small number of single, territory-holding birds (the maximum recorded number was seven in January and February 1967), though it was usually difficult to decide whether they were young birds from the previous summer, non-breeding summering individuals which had shifted their territory, or immigrants. Certainly some young birds remained in the study area until the end of the year and, in a few cases, into January, though most young dispersed out of the study area much earlier. Colour-ringing or wing-tagging would resolve some of these problems but, on the evidence of plumage characteristics, many single wintering birds which set up territories in December or January have come into the area from outside. In addition, between November and March there have been many occurrences of distinctively plumaged individuals which have remained in the forest for up to three weeks without taking up territories before, presumably, moving on. The territories of single birds in winter have similar characteristics to those in summer. They are small, are established in areas vacant of other territories, and the occupants tend to confine themselves to the territory. I have also had the impression, on occasions, that the birds advertise their presence less than do pairs of buzzards in established territories.

In contrast to most single territory-holding, wintering birds, established pairs of buzzards tend to range considerable distances from their territories for food during the winter, though invariably returning to the territory to roost. In October, shortly after, or in some cases coinciding with the dispersal of the young reared that year, there is a period of relatively intensive soaring and display during which confrontations between neighbouring pairs are frequent, marking the re-assertion of territorial boundaries. This intensive territorial behaviour ends early in November—though much depends on the weather—and does not recommence until the second half of February, reaching a climax in the blustery days of March and April. In the intervening months there is relatively little territorial advertisement, either by soaring or boundary perching—indeed, most boundary perches go untenanted for most of the time unless, as occasionally happens, they are used for roosting—and the birds start to travel greater and greater distances in search of prey. Not infrequently I have recorded pairs absent from a territory for up to eight hours at a time, leaving each day to hunt on agricultural land in, or peripheral to, the forest heathlands and woods. I have on several occasions followed (by car) pairs and individual birds as far as four miles from their territory, one pair in particular regularly travelling about that distance to feed on the flood-plain meadows of the Avon valley to the west of the forest.

This extension of hunting range, so evident during the winter, presumably occurs because the agricultural land offers a greater abundance and diversity of prey than the forest, where the populations of woodland birds, which form a major prey source for the New Forest buzzards, are also at their lowest ebb during the year.

Chapter Five

BREEDING BIOLOGY

Most ornithologists who have studied buzzards in Britain and continental Europe have been concerned mainly with the species' numerical status, population density, breeding success and feeding behaviour. This has been inevitable in recent years because such information is of direct relevance to the many who are concerned about the conservation of European raptors. Similarly, in the United States of America, the most recent work on the closely allied red-tailed hawk, which occupies an ecological niche there comparable to that of the buzzard in Europe, has been concerned with food, reproductive success and contamination by pesticide residues.[1] Population studies of buzzards in Britain—such as those of Peter Dare on Dartmoor, and myself in the New Forest—have been concerned only incidentally with those details of breeding biology which can be obtained only by frequent visits to nests, and prolonged and repeated observation at nests throughout the breeding season. In fact, there is seldom time to construct hides and watch individual nests for long periods when one is attempting to obtain quantitative information about the buzzard population in a district the size, say, of the New Forest. In addition, I had the added problem that the public have virtually unrestricted access to the forest, and there was a real risk of hides attracting vandalism and disturbance. Many British bird photographers, however, must have watched the day-to-day events at buzzards' nests, and it is a pity that no one has published accounts of their observations—though I am told that it is impractical to take good photographs and make good observations simultaneously. The other obvious source of information is the nest record card scheme of the British

Trust for Ornithology. Between 1937 and 1969 nearly 900 record cards were filled in by observers in Britain, but although the cards yielded adequate data on clutch size and fledging success, they were otherwise disappointing. Visits to nests, almost without exception, were few and random, and consequently only very incomplete breeding histories were recorded.[2] Not a single card, for example, gave sufficient information from which to calculate the length of the incubation period; and from very few was it possible to determine the length of the fledgling period. There thus remains wide scope for studies of the buzzard's breeding biology, and I would suggest that the species is common enough to justify the risks of disturbance which are inevitably involved.

From the preliminary period of display, starting in late February or early March, to the dispersal of the young from their parents' territory in the autumn, the buzzard's reproductive cycle extends over at least seven months of the year. For at least four of the seven months the focal point of the buzzard's world is the nest.

A thorough search of an established buzzard territory will normally reveal more than one nest, and many territories will possess several. Most of the 43 territories recorded in the New Forest between 1962 and 1971, including all but one (territory 6) of the 27 territories occupied continuously during that time, contained 2 or more nests, though not all the nests found were necessarily occupied during the study period. A total of 138 different nests were found in the 43 territories during the 10 years, giving an average of 3·2 nests per territory. Breeding or attempted breeding (ie the laying of eggs), however, took place in only 98 nests, or an average of 2·3 nests per territory. The data can be analysed further: first, as regards the total numbers of nests per territory. In 8 territories only 1 extant nest was known during the study period; in a further 8 territories only 2 nests were known; in 10 territories 3 nests were known; in 13 territories 4 nests were known; in 2 territories 5 nests were known: in 1 territory, 6 nests were known; and in another territory (territory 2) a relatively close group of no less than 14 nests was found, most of which were felled in 1967, a further 2 nests being built in the succeeding years of the study.

Second, the numbers of nests in each territory actually known to have been used during the study period can be broken down thus: in 12 territories only 1 nest was known to be used for breeding; in 14 territories, 2 nests were known to be used; in 12 territories, 3 nests; in 3 territories, 4 nests; and in 2 territories, 5 nests. All these figures tend to represent the minimum number of nests because, inevitably in densely wooded country, there were undoubtedly in some territories nests used from time to time which were never found. It must also be borne in mind that not all the nests recorded for each territory were necessarily available in each year of the study period—there was a steady, though small, turnover occasioned; on the one hand by losses through disintegration hastened by winter gales, and through timber felling, and on the other hand by the construction of new nests.

The territories with continuous histories of occupation, tended —predictably—to have the large numbers of nests, with the notable exception of one territory in which a pair of buzzards used the same nest for each of the ten years of the study period and had done so for at least three years immediately preceding it—a remarkable record.

The location of nests within New Forest buzzard territories was reasonably predictable, though this did not necessarily mean they were easy to find, especially in the dense canopy of early summer. In a few territories the nests were separated by as much as half a mile, but they would normally be found grouped together within a relatively small area, roughly in the middle of the territory and perhaps about 150 paces in radius. Occasionally a pair would abandon the central group of nests and build and lay in a new and isolated nest at a distance, sometimes quite close to the territory boundary.

The number and distribution of nests in buzzard territories in the New Forest appears to compare closely with buzzard populations elsewhere both in Britain and continental Europe—though my record of 14 nests in a single territory is capped by one writer's comment that 14–15 nests were frequent in buzzard territories in Denmark.[3] In his study area on the edge of Dartmoor, Dare found

29 different nests in 14 buzzard territories.[4] On Skomer, Davis and Saunders recorded 10 different occupied nest sites during the years 1954–64, the buzzard population of the island falling from 8 pairs during 1954 to 4–5 pairs in the early 1960s.[5] A further interesting comparison is with Michael Holdsworth's study of the buzzard population in the Sedbergh area of north-west Yorkshire.[6] Here, on the open fells, buzzard territories appear to be larger than in more varied habitat, and nest sites are often more widely dispersed. Each of seven territories which had consistently supported buzzards between 1937 and 1967 contained more than one nest, and in some cases the nest sites had been in intermittent use throughout the whole of that period and even before. Normally, a pair of buzzards would alternate between two or three nests situated in a group, though in most territories one site seemed to be used more frequently than all the others. Occasionally, however, the regular group of nests would be abandoned in favour of a site on the edge of the territory, a phenomenon already referred to in the New Forest population. As Holdsworth remarked, these 'fringe' sites, which could be 1½ miles from the main group, can easily be overlooked and are clearly exceptions to a general pattern of alternation between two or three nests. He showed that, in the case of the Sedbergh buzzards, the occupation of fringe sites was correlated with the occurrence of good prey (vole) years on the fells. Between 1945 and 1966 there were seven good prey years and ten poor ones. Seven of the recorded occupations of fringe sites occurred in the good years, and only three in the bad; and he suggested that association with familiar sites perhaps becomes less important to the birds when prey is particularly abundant. Put another way, familiarity with the ground around the nest, which must contribute significantly to the hunting success of the adult buzzards, may be less necessary in a good prey year, and a move to fresh ground thus more likely to occur. Unfortunately it has not been possible to demonstrate a similar correlation in the New Forest.

Few of the 98 nests in the New Forest at which pairs of buzzards bred (or attempted to breed) between 1962 and 1971 were occupied in more than two consecutive years, although they were often returned to after a year or two in which an alternative nest or nests were used. In fact, between 1962 and 1971 only eight nests were used in more than two consecutive years. Five nests were used in three consecutive years (in territory 3, 1964–6; territories 7 and 9, 1962–4; and territory 10, 1966–8). One nest (in territory 14) was used in four consecutive years (1967–9); one nest (in territory 38) was used in five consecutive years from 1967, when the territory was first occupied by a pair of buzzards, to the end of the study period; and finally there was the remarkable example of long use mentioned earlier in which the same nest (in territory 6) was used in each year of the study and for at least three years before that. In the Sedbergh area, Holdsworth found that after successful breeding, the chances of a pair of buzzards returning for another season to the same nest or of moving to an alternative, were equal, though it was unusual for a nest to be occupied for more than two successive years. After a breeding failure, however, the chances of the birds moving to a different nest were greatly increased. A not dissimilar phenomenon occurred in the New Forest, though there the chances of reoccupation of the same nest in consecutive years were smaller than on the Sedbergh fells. After 130 successful nestings between 1962 and 1970, the same nest was used in the following year on 54 occasions, 26 of which involved the exceptional examples cited above. Of 23 pairs which laid eggs but failed for various reasons to rear young, only 2 returned to the same nest in the following year. There does not seem to be any obvious reason why the chance of a different nest being used should be increased after a breeding failure, nor, indeed, does there seem to be any convincing general explanation of why buzzards, in common with many other species of raptor, use a number of nests in rotation. Nest sanitation is sometimes invoked, but a winter's exposure to the elements would seem to serve this purpose adequately. In Scottish golden eagles, alternation between a number of nest sites is often associated with regular disturbance, but there seems to be no such correlation in the buzzard.

Buzzards' nests are usually large, solid structures of twigs and small branches up to a foot long, and most nests last a long time.

In the New Forest, and indeed wherever tree nests are usual, they are generally wedged securely in a fork or crotch; but even nests which appear to have been less expertly placed are only occasionally dislodged by winter gales. In the New Forest, at least eight nests still intact in 1971 were then at least fourteen years old, and at least another twenty-four nests were ten years old or more. Added to by the birds over the years, they can become massive. The famous New Forest nest occupied by a breeding pair for 13 consecutive years was about 5ft across and 2½ft deep, and a number of other forest nests achieved a size approaching this. Though I feel certain that the same female laid eggs in this nest for at least 10 of the 13 years (a conviction admittedly based purely on her consistently phlegmatic temperament, for she had no distinguishing plumage characteristics), it is certain that not only territories but individual nests are used by succeeding generations of buzzards, 'knowledge' of the nests presumably being passed on to new birds via the surviving partner of a pair. In some instances, however, nests are probably 're-found'. In two instances in the New Forest, buzzards returned to nests which had been unused for 8 and 10 years respectively, and there were many instances of re-use after gaps of 4 or 5 years. Repeated use by generations of buzzards must be a function of intrinsic site advantages, and these are often difficult for the human observer to evaluate, though regularly used nests generally possess such obvious advantages as ease of access through the canopy, a reasonable field of view, and a degree of shelter. Thus, most such nests were located on the margin of a wood or on the edge of a substantial clearing, the latter often represented in plantations by a large felled area replanted with young trees.

An interesting feature of New Forest buzzard nests was the remarkable consistency with which different nests in the same territory would be found in the same species of tree. In no less than 17 of the 35 territories occupied for five or more years of the study period, nests were exclusively in Scots pine, and almost always 50ft or more up in the crown of a mature tree. In a further territory in which nests were consistently in a similar situation, the birds took to a slender pole crop Douglas fir in a single year. In 6 territories, nests were consistently in mature beech—and in these cases they were sometimes 60–75ft from the ground—one pair in one year, however, abandoning their usual alternative nest sites for a pole crop Scots pine. In 8 territories, nests were consistently in mature oak, 30–50ft up, depending on the stature of the tree, but in 7 instances birds in single years abandoned their normal site type for, in 3 instances, mature Scots pine, in 1 instance a mature larch, in another a huge Weymouth pine, and in 2 others (the same pair in 2 consecutive years) for spindly pole crop Corsican pines. Of the 3 remaining territories making up the total of 35, the nests in 1 were exclusively in mature larch; those in another were in both mature larch and oak; and those in the remaining one were in both mature Scots pine and mature Douglas fir. Most of the occasions when birds deviated from their normal type of site involved the construction of a new nest near the edge of the territory. These were usually small, loosely built and insecurely lodged in the tree, and they seldom survived intact for more than a year or two after use. In one case—one of the nests built in a pole crop Corsican pine—the young birds actually trampled most of the nest through the flimsy branches supporting it, so that towards the end of the fledgling period—but long before they would normally have left the nest for nearby branches—they were left standing precariously on a small vestigial collection of twigs.

Trees appear to be favoured by buzzards for nest sites where they are available. Dare found a predilection for Scots pine on Dartmoor, similar to that of buzzards in the New Forest. Elsewhere, hedgerow oaks and ash and, more occasionally, isolated hawthorn bushes or alder carr are used. In relatively treeless country, nest sites on cliffs, crags, quarry faces and the sides of ravines are normal. Table 3[7] analyses by regions the situations of buzzards' nests recorded on 874 British Trust for Ornithology nest record cards between 1937 and 1969, though it must be recognised that the figures give only a general indication of the frequency with which different types of site were used in different regions because they refer to the numbers of cards and not the numbers of nests: many cards clearly referred to the same nest in different years. Nevertheless the table does suggest that the use of nest sites other than in woodland tends to be a matter of necessity rather than of inherent preference. The largest number of crag, cliff or quarry face nests was recorded from the comparatively treeless northern Pennines and Lakeland. Most of the sea cliff nests were recorded from Pembrokeshire, where alternatives are few. All the hedgerow and isolated tree sites were in Wales and the South-west Peninsula, and here it is possible that they represented secondary choices made necessary by the capacity occupation of the more favoured areas containing woodland. The numbers of hedgerow nest sites is particularly interesting because it lends support to the notion that buzzards could spread back into much of lowland agricultural England where woods are comparatively scarce, if once they were given the chance.

TABLE 3

Situations of buzzards' nests recorded on 874 British Trust for Ornithology nest record cards 1937–69

Region	*Tree in woodland*	*Isolated or hedge-row tree*	*Inland crag, cliff or quarry*	*Sea cliff*
New Forest	158			
SW England	45	27	1	2
Wales & the Marches	103	38	17	53
NW England	84		168	
Scottish Highlands	117		50	2
S Uplands, Scotland	3		1	
Antrim				2
Surry/Sussex	2			

In the New Forest, buzzards begin to add fresh material to their nests as early as the middle of February if the weather is mild. By the third week of March at the latest, at least one, and often two or even three nests in each occupied territory are likely to have been decorated with green sprays. Nest decoration is invariably of twigs and small branches torn from the living tree and woven, usually rather insecurely, into the structure of the nest—at first Scots pine, then larch, and later, as they come into leaf, oak and beech; though ivy, birch and ash may also be used, and elsewhere various other species have been recorded—and also, on the coast, seaweed. The main structure of a freshly built nest, on the other hand, is mainly dead material.

Nest decoration is associated especially with the initial period of intensive display and, as I suggested in Chapter Four, it may conceivably have some function associated with the pair-bond and courtship—certainly the material added to nests early in the season is seldom of any practical use and much of it usually finds its way to the ground. Display flights in which the male carries a spray often terminate—or perhaps culminate—in the descent of the pair into the tree canopy, and possibly this may be followed by some sort of nest adornment ceremony. Unfortunately I have never actually witnessed a buzzard adding to a nest during the pre-incubation period, though I have occasionally watched one bring a spray to the nest from a nearby tree later in the breeding season—sprays continue to be added to occupied nests throughout the incubation period and for much, sometimes for most, of the fledgling period. The habit, however, is not actually invariable, and I have occasionally known buzzards' nests from which young have been reared that have not exhibited a vestige of decoration.

Not only will more than one nest in a territory be decorated with green sprays early in the season, but more than one will often be structurally 'patched up' and even freshly lined during March and April. Moreover, fresh sprays often continue to be added—probably by the male, though I have never witnessed the event—to 'spare' nests long after eggs have been laid—occasionally well into the fledgling period. Of 178 records of breeding in the New Forest between 1962 and 1971, there were thirty-five instances in which this behaviour was recorded, and this figure is certainly a minimal one because in many other cases in which occupied nests were known, other nests in the territory were not examined. Other writers, both in Britain and in continental Europe, have alluded to the habit, which is shared by some other large raptors and can possibly be explained as a form of advertisement of territory ownership, though this interpretation has more credibility in open hill country where the nests are on exposed crags than in wooded areas such as the New Forest. From the point of view of the human observer searching the woods or fells it can give rise to much doubt and confusion at times and it is well to beware suggestions of non-breeding based only on the finding of lined and decorated, but unused, nests—the behaviour of the adults needs to be taken into account and a thorough search of the territory is usually necessary before failure to breed can be established with reasonable certainty—and I have been caught out once or twice even after that. Decorated nests were found early in the season in most of the thirty-seven instances in which I was satisfied that pairs failed to breed in the New Forest between 1962 and 1971. In fourteen of the thirty-seven instances, nests which were structurally repaired and relined during April continued to be added to throughout May and most of June; and in a further four instances nests which had been decorated in an apparently desultory way in March were suddenly repaired, relined and decorated in late May or early June.

The reconstruction and relining of old nests or the construction of new nests in which eggs are to be laid is normally complete early in April in the New Forest, though laying may be delayed a further week or two. I have never witnessed the construction of a nest, but this can be accomplished in a remarkably short time. Chance has twice led me to newly built nests in trees which had not held the vestige of one just two days previously, and it seems probable that most of the material is collected from the immediate vicinity of the tree. In the New Forest, nest linings are commonly of spruce tips. Elsewhere, a variety of other material has been recorded, including dead bracken, bark, dead grass (usually purple moor grass, when it has been identified), Scots pine needles and, at sea cliff nests, seaweeds.

Determining the dates at which egg laying commences in any reasonably large sample of buzzard nests from a particular area is by no means easy. The only certain way of obtaining this information is to make day-to-day examinations of the nests throughout the critical period, and for various reasons—notably limitations of time and difficulties of access to nests, especially when they are in high trees or on cliff faces—this is seldom possible (certainly not for a large sample). From data obtained later in the breeding season, such as the dates on which eggs were found hatching, or clutches found partly hatched, or the estimated age of small young, it is possible to calculate laying dates, but such calculations can only be regarded as approximations because there are uncertainties about the precise length of the incubation period, which in any case probably varies within at least narrow limits.

Eggs have been consistently recorded as being laid at intervals of 3 days both in Britain and continental Europe, and observers in Germany have reported an incubation period of 33 days for the first egg, the remaining eggs hatching at further intervals of 2 days each.[8] Clutches mostly vary in size between 2 and 4 eggs (see Chapter Six) and incubation, as in many raptors, starts with the laying of the first egg.

In the only instance in 10 years in the New Forest when the exact laying and hatching dates were known, the first egg of a clutch of 2 was found at 19·00 hours on the evening of 19 April 1964; the clutch was complete at 19·30 hours on the evening of 21 April (suggesting that the first egg had been laid on 18 April if an interval of 3 days between eggs is allowed); and in the afternoon of the 24 May the nest held a chick still emerging from the egg and an egg which had not yet started chipping. The incubation period of the first egg was thus 36 days. Unfortunately the nest could not be revisited for a further week after the 24 May so that the hatching interval between eggs was not determined.

In Cornwall, B. H. Ryves obtained data from 2 nests. Eggs were laid at 3-day intervals. In one nest the incubation period was 38 days for the first egg and 36 days for the other egg of the clutch. In the second nest it was 37 days for the first egg; 36 days for the second egg; and 34 days for the third egg.[9] Thus, from the fragmentary data available there seems to be some variation in the length of incubation period, complicated also by variations associated with asynchronous laying and hatching.

Assuming an incubation period of 36 days for the first egg, a laying interval of 3 days between eggs and a hatching interval of 2 days between eggs, the approximate laying dates of the first egg in 49 nests in the New Forest between 1962 and 1971 can be calculated from the dates on which nests were later found with young and unhatched eggs, or with young the age of which could be estimated with confidence. The earliest calculated laying date was 6–8 April and the latest was 4–6 May. The median laying date was 18 April. All but 8 clutches were laid between 10 April and 26 April.

How does this compare with elsewhere? In Cornwall, B. H. Ryves found from twenty-five years experience that buzzards laid between 9 and 20 April, only a small proportion laying after the latter date. In Somerset, the Rev C. J. Pringle recorded a slightly later laying period, between 15 and 25 April, which was similar to that given by Bruce Campbell for Argyll. On the edge of Dartmoor, Peter Dare found that most of his study population laid between 6 and 25 April, with occasional records of birds laying as late as the second week of May. Further north, in Lakeland, R. H. Brown considered clutches completed by around 21 April to be early, and R. A. H. Coombes considered that most Lakeland buzzards laid during the days 19–29 April, but agreed that complete clutches were unusual before 21 April. Coombes' earliest records of complete Lakeland clutches were on 14 April 1932 and 15 April 1938. More recently Michael Holdsworth has calculated the median laying date for the first egg of buzzards in the Sedbergh area of Yorkshire as 21 April, with a range from 8 April to 9 May. The calculations involved the use of data similar to that used for the New Forest but assuming a 33-day incubation period—which would make his median data a little late if the longer incubation period of 36 or more days is assumed to be valid for north-west Yorkshire.[10] Data from the British Trust for Ornithology nest record cards suggest that in the Scottish Highlands laying dates may be slightly later than further south, though the only cards which provided definite information were one from Banff, which gave a calculated laying date of 27 April for the first egg, assuming a 36-day incubation period; and two from Inverness-shire, which suggested laying dates of around 21 April. In the absence of more comprehensive information, all that can be said is that there is comparatively little latitudinal difference in laying dates in Britain, which is not unexpected considering the relatively small variation in spring temperatures down the Atlantic side of Britain populated by buzzards. In north-west Europe, laying dates are somewhat earlier than in Britain, and T. Mebs, for example, calculated the median laying date for 62 nests over a 5-year period in Germany as 10 April.[11]

In Britain, buzzards normally lay 2–3 eggs, though the number can range between 1 and—exceptionally—6. Both sexes take part in incubation, though the greater share falls to the female, and indeed, in some instances in the New Forest I have strongly suspected that incubation was completed entirely by the female. Certainly she is tied closely to the nest throughout incubation and for the first 3 weeks after the eggs hatch. During this period of about 8½ weeks most females appear to make few kills, the male alone providing most of the food—a considerable test of his hunting efficiency unless prey is especially abundant. Behaviour during incubation varies somewhat from pair to pair and, possibly, it may also vary from year to year according to the availability of prey. My own observations at buzzards' nests in the New Forest, though limited in scope, certainly tend to confirm that there is individual variation both in behaviour and temperament of different pairs.

Buzzards are relatively easy to watch at the nest without the paraphernalia of a hide, providing the observer is content to remain at a distance. In the New Forest I found that if I sat quietly at the foot of a tree about 50yd from that which held the nest, the birds would in most cases ignore me, though they must usually have been aware of my presence. Watching in this manner, of course, has its limitations, not the least of which is the difficulty often encountered in obtaining a clear view of the nest (and, of course, one cannot see its interior); but it can nevertheless be rewarding. Some pairs proved more cautious than others, and sometimes individual birds—invariably males if the sex was determined—refused to approach the nest whilst I remained watching it, whilst other individuals

ge 135 (*right*) Typical crag
t; (*below*) adult arriving at
t with rabbit—large prey
ms usually arrive in the talons.
e young are 4–5 weeks old

Page 136 (*left*) Six-week old young on nest;
(*below*) wing exercise—young buzzard about 7 weeks old

exhibited less acute, but nevertheless equally clear, signs of nervousness. To continue watching in such circumstances was quite pointless and was always abandoned since behaviour was likely to be atypical even if the birds did eventually appear to overcome some of their caution. On the other hand, some pairs seemed remarkably tolerant of an observer and would go about their business unconcerned even by sudden movement or noise, such as might occur when a persistent mosquito finally presented a satisfactory target.

Between 1962 and 1967 I spent a total of about 220 hours watching at 10 different buzzard's nests in the New Forest, of which about 45 hours watching at 6 nests was during the incubation period. Most of the watching during incubation was in spells of about three hours, which is really too short a period to obtain adequate information about the frequency with which the non-incubating bird visited the nest, about the sharing of incubation between the sexes, or about other behavioural questions. In 12 out of 16 spells of watching, all before 11·00 hours, a second adult visited the nest at least once and on some occasions remained in the vicinity of the nest for a considerable part of the watch. Despite this record of activity, watching at nests during incubation could tax the patience. For most of the time all that one was likely to see was the tail, and sometimes the head, of the sitting bird, immobile on the nest. Occasionally there would be a movement as she shifted her position or, perhaps, turned the eggs—usually it was difficult to see exactly what was happening from the ground—and sometimes she might be seen re-arranging nest material or decorative sprays. The appearance of the second bird was sometimes heralded by a short, rather low-pitched 'ca . . . ow' call, almost a yelp, though equally as often the first intimation of its approach to the human observer (apart from the sudden alertness of the sitting bird) would be the appearance of a brown form sweeping through the canopy on to the branch of a nearby tree, there to transfer prey from talons to bill before pitching on the nest itself. The visit to the nest would be unmarked by ceremony, the male simply dropping the prey on the nest, standing on its edge for a minute or two at most, and then departing as abruptly as it had arrived. Once, the incubating bird responded to its mate's approach call by leaving the nest, probably to take the prey among the trees nearby. Twice, following the male's visit to the nest with prey, the female departed for a while, the prey left neglected behind her. She did not go far, however, for on both occasions I caught glimpses of one or both birds among the surrounding trees. After one of these excursions the (presumed) female returned to the nest with a fresh green spray of beech. There were two other occasions, both in the early morning, when I watched the incubating bird leave the nest and return after a short while with fresh greenery, and another when both birds arrived at the nest with fresh sprays within a few seconds of each other.

Determining the roles played by the sexes in incubation is difficult unless there happen to be clear plumage differences between the two birds. It is usually difficult, if not impossible, to distinguish the sexes by the usual field characters in the uncertain light beneath the canopy, especially when views are relatively brief or, worse, confined to a head or tail just visible over the rim of a nest. However, during the forty-five hours observation at nests during the incubation period, and in many more hours casual watching, I never witnessed a nest relief and, assuming the male always to be the bird bringing prey to the nest, I have no certain record of a male buzzard incubating eggs. It should, however, be remembered that my observations at nests extended over only a few hours and, moreover, were confined to the periods of the day when most hunting is done and when the male would be least likely to participate in incubation.

In sum, my own fragmentary observations at nests in the New Forest during incubation support the findings of other observers in suggesting that the female seldom moves far from the nest at this time and that the male provides most, perhaps in some cases, all her food. Two buzzards soaring together over a territory during May or early June are likely to be a non-breeding pair or one occupant of the territory 'seeing off' an intruder from another. It is not often that one can identify a male and female buzzard soaring together at this time if the territory contains a nest with viable eggs.

Because incubation starts with the laying of the first egg, the young hatch asynchronously, generally at intervals of about forty-eight hours, and until the brood is well feathered the oldest birds remain readily distinguishable by their size and more advanced plumage. Most clutches hatch in the New Forest between about 20 May and the end of the month. On hatching, young buzzards weigh about 40–45g, but by the beginning of their third week of life they may weigh ten times that weight, which is nearly half that of a healthy adult buzzard—an adult male is likely to weigh around 850g, and an adult female 100–150g more. By their fifth week the chicks are likely to have doubled their weight again, so that they are by then almost the weight of an adult. After that, however, there is little further weight increment, food being converted to feather production. In the New Forest most young buzzards ventured from the nest on to nearby branches for the first time during their seventh week, and made their first flights anything from two or three days to a week or more later. Since they return to the nest for a variable period after first leaving it—indeed, at first the adults continue to bring their food to the nest, and they sometimes roost on it at night—it is not easy to assign a definite length to the fledgling period. The length of the fledgling period in the New Forest—that is, the time between hatching and first flight —varied between 47 and 57 days. In 12 cases (ie of one young bird each) in which it was known precisely, the average was 55 days, which agrees well with Peter Dare's estimate of 53 days for his Dartmoor population. It may be another six or eight weeks or even longer before the young are independent of their parents for food.

For the first few days after hatching, the chicks are brooded more or less continuously by the female, and they are two weeks old or more before she leaves them for long. During this early part of the fledgling period the male has to find enough prey for the whole family and, indeed, not until the young are about four weeks old does the female make a major contribution to the hunting effort—though in the third and fourth weeks of the chicks' lives she will bring prey to the nest from time to time, most of it probably caught nearby. Thus, the female remains at or close to the nest throughout the period when the young are in down and, presumably, most vulnerable to cold and wet (the onset of rain will invariably bring her to the nest to shelter them) and to casual predation by corvids. By the time the young buzzards are four weeks old, however, they are comparatively large, active, and well feathered, and they are left very much to themselves on the nest, the visits of the adults becoming progressively briefer.

For the first two weeks of their lives the young buzzards are fed by the female, who tears up and distributes to them the prey brought to the nest by the male. Twice I have watched a female buzzard disgorging what must have been partly masticated meat to young a few days old, but my observations at nests have been too limited during the early days of the fledgling period to determine if this is then a regular habit. In their third week the young start to pick and tear inexpertly at carcases left on the nest, and thereafter rapidly learn to feed themselves. There is clearly a 'knack' to dismembering a carcase using a hooked bill, for the early efforts of young buzzards sometimes leave the impression that the meat is the consistency of rubber. This is especially so with frogs, and it is easy to imagine chagrin in the attitudes struck by a young buzzard when, for the umpteenth time, the frog, held down by a talon and wrenched at with the bill, stretches and then contracts suddenly like a piece of elastic. By the time they are a month old, however, they have learnt to swallow frogs and small rodents whole, and are becoming practised in shredding larger items of prey.

Watching buzzards at their nests when they have young is vastly more entertaining than when they are incubating eggs, because there is more activity to watch, and it must be confessed that it was partly for this reason that most of my nest observation in the New Forest took place after the young had hatched, though a more objective purpose was to obtain information about prey species and the frequency with which the adults brought prey to the nest. A total of 175 hours was spent watching at 10 nests between 1962 and 1967, usually in spells of between two and four hours and mainly between 06·00 and 11·00 hours and again in the evening. Feeding was most frequent at all stages of the fledgling period during the early morning, from first light to around 10·00 hours (though observations before 06·00 were few, for obvious and unscientific reasons), and again after 18·00 hours, adults sometimes bringing in prey when it was almost too dark to see among the trees. The adult buzzards' hunting day in the fledgling period is thus a long one, extending over about eighteen hours at midsummer in the south of England and, presumably, even longer further north. In Dare's Dartmoor population the male buzzards were active from dawn to dusk in summer, and for most of the time (8½ out of 11 hours in one case, and 11½ out of 13½ hours in another) they were actually hunting. That a good deal of avian prey was caught in the half light at either end of the day in the New Forest was suggested not only from observations actually at nests but from more casual sightings of birds hunting, sparrowhawk-fashion, among the crowns of the trees and along woodland margins at those times. The early morning—though some time after sunlight (if the sun had appeared) had started to filter through the canopy—was also a likely time for the renewal of the sprays decorating the nest, the female, and very occasionally the male, returning several times within an hour with fresh material collected nearby.

Unfortunately I was never able to watch continuously at nests for entire days, but nevertheless it was possible from the cumulative experience of watching at different times of the day, to estimate very approximately the frequency with which prey was delivered at different stages in the growth of the young; though it must be appreciated that frequency is likely to be related to the weight of individual prey items brought to the nest, and can thus be expected to vary widely in the New Forest buzzard population which feeds on a wide variety of prey species.

In the first week of the fledgling period, a female brooding two small young could expect to be visited by the male at least six and probably eight or more times a day if the prey was small mammals (mostly wood mice in the New Forest), small passerine birds, or frogs, but on far fewer occasions if the prey was larger—say, young rabbits, grey squirrels or large birds. In the second and third weeks the male would be likely to visit the nest with small items of prey a dozen or more times a day. In the early morning (before 08·00 hours) the male buzzard would sometimes return at about half-hour intervals, usually with wood mice, frogs or small birds, but during the main part of the day, from about 09·00 to 18·00 hours, he might make only two or three visits. Rabbits and other heavy items were invariably delivered in the talons, but smaller prey was generally transferred to the bill before the final approach to the nest. Sometimes a female would leave the nest to receive prey from the male a short distance away.

By the beginning of the fourth week of the fledgling period the pressure on the male as the provider of food would be eased and, though the total number of visits to the nest with prey would tend to increase slightly after that, perhaps half or more of these would be made by the female. Indeed, at one nest containing month-old young I saw the male (a distinctively pale and clearly identifiable bird) arrive with prey only twice compared with eight visits by the female. They may merely have been fortuitous, but it is possible that the male sometimes actually adopts a secondary role in providing food for the young late in the fledgling period.

Deaths among the brood are not uncommon and occur almost entirely during the second, third and fourth weeks of the fledgling period. The adult buzzards make no attempt to ensure a fair distribution of the available food among their offspring, and the older birds, being heavier and more active, tend to take most of the prey delivered at the nest, often physically resisting the younger birds in obtaining it. All is well so long as the adults can make a sufficient number of kills to satisfy the food requirements of the whole brood, for the smaller birds will then have their share after the larger ones have become glutted and torpid. If, however, insufficient prey is available or it is difficult to catch, the smaller and weaker young may starve, their demise sometimes hastened by the deliberate attacks of their older brethren. The corpses of those which thus perish are eaten by the surviving member or members of the brood and may, indeed, be dismembered and fed to them by the adults.

Losses among broods are not always obviously related to food supply. In 1965, for example, P. J. Panting recorded comparatively large-scale losses of young from nests in central Wales, where broods of two or three young had in most cases been reduced to a single youngster during the first two weeks of the fledgling period, though there was an abundance of prey available and a surplus of prey items on nests. A nest examined on 11 June, for example, held two large downy young and one small one. When the nest was visited on 13 June only one of the two larger birds survived, the remaining two having gone without trace—presumably eaten. On both occasions there were numerous prey items on the nest, and Peter Panting suggested that some losses occur when the young become wet during continuous rain and perhaps contract pneumonia—suggesting in turn that the female may not always cover the young very efficiently.[12]

On the assumption that high rainfall would tend to reduce the hunting success of the adult buzzards and thus increase the chances of brood depletion from starvation, or alternatively, increase the likelihood of the young contracting pneumonia, I compared the annual output of young buzzards in the New Forest during 1962–71 with the annual May and June rainfall. It was not, however, possible to establish any adverse relationship, and certainly rain, however continuous, does not actually prevent buzzards hunting. Indeed, if rainfall affects breeding success it is remarkable that Welsh buzzards rear young at all.

In Inverness-shire, in 1962, L. MacNally recorded the older of a brood of two as killing the younger on a nest laden with prey. On 8 June, when the older bird was about sixteen days old and able to pick shreds from a rabbit lying on the nest, it savagely repulsed the young chick when it attempted to do the same. During the following week this aggressiveness increased, even when there was plenty of food on the nest. On the morning of 15 June the head of the younger chick was criss-crossed with red cuts, and by 18·00 hours the same day it was dead—surrounded by an abundance of food.[13]

I have seen similar head injuries on the smallest members of some New Forest broods, though it was always my impression that the victim was already in a state of advanced starvation before it suffered physical damage, and there was never a surplus of prey on the nest.

On Dartmoor, Peter Dare thought that the second week of the fledgling period was the most critical for the survival of the whole brood, and this seems logical because at that time the young are starting to grow rapidly and to demand a substantial weight of food, whilst the female has not yet started to assist the male in providing it. The critical period in the New Forest, however, seems to be somewhat later, immediately after the female has ceased to shelter or brood the young and is starting to hunt for prey. The age at which the young died was known to within two or three days in sixteen cases of brood depletion in the New Forest between 1962 and 1971, and in all but three of these the losses occurred when the oldest of the brood was in its third or fourth week—which in most cases was within a week either side of 15 June. Of the three exceptions, one was a brood of two, of which one young died in its second week of life, and the remaining two were broods of single young found dead on the nest when only two or three days old. Both these latter incidents occurred in 1971 in adjacent territories and, interestingly, they were the only records of total brood failure during the whole of my study. In one case, only a leg of the young bird was found, and in the other a decapitated body, suggesting that the corpses had been partially eaten by the adults. It is tempting to speculate that the young starved because of a locally catastrophic decline in prey resources, although there was no evidence to support this, and both broods may coincidentally have succumbed for other reasons, of which predation by crows is perhaps the most likely.

It is difficult to account for the timing of brood depletion in the New Forest in terms of availability of prey. Most young buzzards hatch towards the end of May, and the first three or four weeks of their lives coincide with the appearance of large numbers of inexperienced young jackdaws and other medium-sized passerine birds, on which New Forest buzzards extensively depend. It may be, however, that by mid-June, when brood depletion mainly occurs, the demands of the young buzzards for an increasing amount of food daily tend to outstrip the ability of the adults to catch sufficient avian prey in a situation in which alternative food sources are inadequate. Some pairs of buzzards depend heavily on young jackdaws, and by mid-June these are not only growing in experience and ability to evade capture but are also feeding away from the colonial breeding sites in the old beech woods, so that the hunting success of the buzzards may be reduced below a threshold which is significant for the survival of their smaller offspring.

Asynchronous hatching (and its consequence for the smallest of the brood) occurs in many species of raptors and corvids and, as J. D. Lockie showed for some corvids, can be regarded as a means by which the number of young is adjusted to the available food supply when this is variable and the fledgling period is long.[14] This view, however, does not entirely conform with Dare's observations on his Dartmoor buzzard population, where the critical factor affecting the survival of the smallest of the brood seems to have been the part played by the female in seeking prey rather than variations in actual prey-biomass. The phenomenon of brood depletion in the buzzard would also bear further examination in the light of records of young birds dying in situations of apparent food abundance.

Brood depletion after the young buzzards are about five weeks old seems to be rare—I knew of not a single example in the New Forest in ten years—presumably because not only are both adults hunting, but the weight increment of the young tends to decline as they achieve adult stature. At the end of the fledgling period, during the week or ten days before they leave the nest, the frequency with which prey is brought to the young definitely declines. Fully feathered, save for their short primary, secondary and tail feathers, and with perhaps a trace of down remaining on the head, they are left to their own devices for hours at a time, clambering about the nest, indulging in wing-flapping exercises which sometimes threaten to make them prematurely airborne, and attacking in an apparently desultory way whatever prey there is on the nest. At this time, and for some time after they leave the nest, they are very vocal, the otherwise silent woods ringing to their repeated 'Ksee . . . ooh' calls, longer, drawn-out, shrill versions of the adults' voices, audible at a considerable distance and very helpful in searching for nests late in the season—so helpful that one wonders what function the habit has. Certainly the calls are not necessarily associated with food-soliciting (though after the young have left the nest they possibly serve as a 'homing' device for an adult with food) and indeed, prey brought to the nest by the adults seldom receives the voracious attentions that it would have received earlier in the fledgling period, and nor does the visit of an adult with prey always still the strident voices of the young buzzards.

How soon the young leave the nest depends largely on its situation. If, for example, it is in a big beech with plenty of convenient limbs on to which the young can climb directly from the nest, they may venture forth early in their seventh week. If the tree is close to others into which the young can launch themselves without meeting the resistance of dense foliage, then they may fly for the first time before they are seven weeks old. If, on the other hand, the nest is perched in a relatively isolated pine which also lacks lateral branches, the young may not leave until they are 8–8½ weeks old, then to launch themselves directly into space.

After fledging, the adults continue to bring food to the nest for some time, the young returning there as a parent approaches. The young also sometimes roost on the nest, though this is probably less deliberate than fortuitous in the sense that they merely remain there after a late evening delivery of prey.

Though the period of attachment to the actual nest after fledging may be fairly short, the young remain remarkably close to it—usually within about 300yd—for some weeks. The period of the breeding-cycle from fledging to autumn dispersal is perhaps the most mysterious because the focal point of the nest is lost to the observer. The growth of wing and tail feathers is probably not complete for two or three weeks after the first tentative flight, but how much longer elapses before the young birds first kill for themselves is simply not known. Certainly they are fed by the adults for 6–8 weeks, sometimes longer. At first they rise out of the canopy on unsteady, winnowing wings, and with excited calls to greet the parent approaching with food, following it and its burden back into the trees and on to the nest. Later, when they are stronger on the wing, the young will pursue a food-carrying adult up into a soar, calling continually, and I have sometimes watched what appeared to be a deliberate attempt at a food pass, the adult releasing the prey from its talons, and the young birds tumbling earthwards after it. When—and how—they learn to kill is a matter for conjecture, but it would seem reasonable to suppose that they are encouraged to do so by the waning enthusiasm of the adults for supplying them with food, which becomes very evident after the middle of August, when the appearance of adult buzzards with food becomes progressively less frequent. By the time the young have been fledged for six weeks, they receive food from the adults only sporadically.

I have watched young buzzards hunting, or attempting to hunt, from observation posts in early September. On the other hand I have occasionally seen an adult carrying prey to young birds in the third week of that month. Thus the transition from being supported to being self-supporting is gradual, and occurs during a period extending from mid-August to middle or late September. In the New Forest most broods still remain in their parents' territory at the end of September and many, perhaps most, are still there a month later, though it is very difficult to obtain a good census of young buzzards in heavily wooded country like the forest. Few young, however, remain by the middle of November —though I have occasionally seen adults and young circling together over the nest site in mid-December, the calls of the young still a little shrill and juvenile. Clearly there is no question of the adults attempting to drive their offspring away (nor is there any convincing evidence of this occurring in other raptors, though it apparently does so in some owls) and it seems that they eventually drift off on their own initiative.

The newly fledged young buzzards look much like the adults

except that the underside of the body appears either uniformly brown, or blotched, rather than barred, whilst the mantle, scapulars and covert feathers have pale edgings. The crown of the head, too, is often lightly streaked with white, which is not usual in an adult. Few of these distinguishing features, however, are of use at a distance in the field and, indeed, even at close range some juvenile buzzards are indistinguishable from adults. For the first few weeks during which they are on the wing, however, they are readily separated from their parents by their silhouette and movement in flight. They appear to have longer and narrower wings than the adults, presumably because the secondary feathers (ie those along the trailing edge of the wing) have not completed their growth; and when they soar, the wings are held more or less level with the body instead of being tilted rigidly upwards at a slight angle. Also, of course, they 'look' young, their movements betraying inexperience. By the end of September, however, it is seldom possible to separate young from adults on field characters alone, and once the juvenile feathers have become abraded they are less and less easy to distinguish by plumage at close range. The juvenile plumage is moulted during the spring, summer and autumn of the following year. It is probably another year before the young buzzards—or those which have survived—are able to breed.

I should like to conclude this chapter by considering in a speculative way the prey-biomass necessary to support a successful breeding pair of buzzards.

First, what is the daily food requirement of an adult buzzard? Kai Curry-Lindahl gave an average of 170g/day for captive buzzards at Skansen, the Zoological Gardens of Stockholm,[15] and O. Uttendörfer gave an average of 150g/day in his book on the food of birds of prey in Europe.[16] These figures, however, exceed 10 per cent of the body weight of an adult buzzard, and may well be excessive for wild adult birds. J. J. and F. C. Craighead calculated that captive American buzzards consumed 8–10 per cent of their body weight per day,[17] and it seems better to accept this figure as a starting-point for tentative calculations. Thus, a buzzard is likely to require something of the order of 70–100g of food each day, and a pair of buzzards will require of the order of 51–73kg each year. Dare, using a figure of 140g/day, or roughly 16 per cent of the body weight of an adult male buzzard, arrived at a figure of 101kg/pair/year, which—subjectively—I suspect is high.

More important, Dare was able to calculate, from prey recovered at the nest, the approximate demands of the young at different stages of the fledgling period. He calculated that the food requirement of each chick was made up of: 50g/day in days 1–5; 85g/day in days 6–14; 130g/day in days 15–21; 165g/day in days 22–42; and 150g/day in days 43–52. Using these figures, and assuming that the food requirements of the young fall after fledging to approximately that of an adult, and allowing a period of ten weeks after fledging, a pair of buzzards rearing two young would require approximately 80–100kg of food per year. This compares with Dare's calculation of approximately 130kg.

These figures become more meaningful when they are interpreted in terms of numbers of prey items. My figure of 100kg could be made up, for example, of about 400 young rabbits each weighing 250g; or about 3,300 short-tailed voles each weighing 30g; or about 1,100 moles each weighing 90g; or about 650 jackdaws each weighing about 150g. Over most of the buzzard's range in Britain and continental Europe small mammals now make up the bulk of its prey, and assuming 20g as a reasonable median weight for all small mammals—voles, mice and shrews—a pair of buzzards rearing two young would need about 5,000 a year. Dare, using his figure of 130kg/pair/year, suggested that a pair of buzzards inhabiting a territory for a year and rearing two young would eat the equivalent of approximately 580 young rabbits or 7,000 adult voles or mice.

In terms of its daily food requirement it will be evident that a buzzard will have more than enough to eat if it catches a single young rabbit, whereas it might alternatively have to catch as many as five small mammals. In fact, it is likely that an adult buzzard can survive on substantially less than 70–100g/day and, indeed, can go without food altogether for several days at a time during a grave winter food shortage. In spring and summer, however, not only must the brood be fed regularly, but the energy expended in increased hunting activity presumably increases the food demands of the adults as well. Table 4 attempts to interpret the prey requirements of a pair of buzzards and their brood of two young at

TABLE 4

Prey requirements of a pair of buzzards with two young in the fledgling period

Day	Weight of prey required (g)	Numbers of alternative prey species required					
		Young rabbit (250g)	Voles (30g)	Young grey squirrel (350g)	Moles (90g)	Jackdaw (150g)	Young woodpigeon (350g)
1–5	300	2	10	1	3–4	2	1
6–14	370	2	12–13	1–2	4–5	3	1
15–21	460	2	15–16	1–2	5–6	3–4	2
22–42	530	3	17–18	1–2	6	4	2
43–52	500	2	16–17	1–2	6	4	2

different stages of the fledgling period. Accepting the somewhat arbitrary nature of the weight estimates involved, the table is nevertheless illuminating and emphasises first, the heavy demands made on the male early in the fledgling period before the female is hunting regularly, in areas where small mammals are the main source of food; and second, why the buzzard can maintain high density populations, and rear large broods in areas where rabbits are plentiful. To feed himself, his mate, and a brood of three in the second week of the fledgling period, the male buzzard might have to kill as many as fifteen or sixteen times a day, or a little less than once every hour—a doubtfully possible achievement. On the other hand if rabbits are available he need kill only twice or perhaps three times a day.

Though fewer birds than small mammals would be required,

they probably require more time and skill to catch. In the absence of abundant rodents, however, New Forest buzzards depend heavily on birds, at least during the breeding season. The buzzard population there may be remarkable in this respect, but it does confirm that the buzzard can adapt to circumstances very different to those with which most observers of the species are familiar. Predictably, however, the output of young birds from the New Forest is low compared with areas where rabbits and voles are abundant—a situation which is explored further in Chapter Six.

Chapter Six

POPULATION ECOLOGY

The versatility of the buzzard as a predator and its capacity for adapting to a variety of prey and habitat situations were emphasised in the opening chapter. In the absence of deliberate persecution by man these characteristics make for a widespread and successful species, but nevertheless it is apparent that—persecution apart—the numbers of buzzards and the success with which they rear young can be influenced by various factors of which the most important is, perhaps, the availability of prey, which in turn may be a function of more general environmental conditions. Because of their position at the end of the food chain, raptors are often useful barometers of environmental changes, and most studies of raptors during the past decade or more have concentrated on the measurement of populations and their reproduction. My own study of the buzzard population of the New Forest was no exception. The changing fortunes of the buzzard population of Britain, and to some extent, its breeding success, was charted in Chapters Two and Three. The first intention in this final chapter is to focus more closely on the breeding success of buzzards in Britain in recent years, and to compare information obtained from parts of the country between which there may be differences in habitat and prey resources. In conclusion it is intended to consider what happens to the young buzzards reared each year. Where do they go after they disperse from their parents' territories? How many survive to breed? How much do we know about the balance between mortality and recruitment in buzzard populations? In sum, this chapter is essentially concerned with the production and the destiny of young buzzards.

During my study of the New Forest buzzards it became apparent that the average clutch size and the output of young there was consistently lower than appeared (from either my own experiences or those of other observers) to be usual further west and north in Britain, and this prompted me to analyse the British Trust for Ornithology nest record cards for the species in order to explore these regional differences. At the same time it seemed logical to see if the cards threw up any long-term regional or national trends in breeding success.[1]

The ideal measure of breeding success is the number of young birds reared by a known population of adults, but unfortunately the proportion of non-breeding adults in a population is seldom known. Breeding success is thus more often measured by the number of young reared by a given number of pairs which bred or attempted to breed. The other statistics important to an understanding of population success are the size of clutches laid and the numbers of young which hatch. Nest records were completed only for nests in which breeding was actually attempted, and figures derived from the cards cannot, therefore, take into account the non-breeding populations of territory-holding adults. The cards suffered from the further limitations that the numbers completed and returned annually to the BTO were small, and that comparatively few cards recorded complete histories of nests—information about hatching success being particularly inadequate. Despite these limiations, however, the cards yielded some interesting information to complement the few detailed local studies of buzzard populations which have been undertaken in Britain.

The earliest nest record cards were for 1937 (from Westmorland) and my analysis covered the years up to and including 1969. A total of 874 cards yielded information about clutch size and fledging success, 852 referring to the period 1948–69 and only 22—mostly from Westmorland and north-west Yorkshire—to earlier years. It was not until 1948 that the annual total achieved double figures. Not until 1964 did it exceed 50. The largest number returned in any one year was 91 cards in 1968. Not only were the annual totals small but, as will be seen from Fig 9, which shows the numbers of

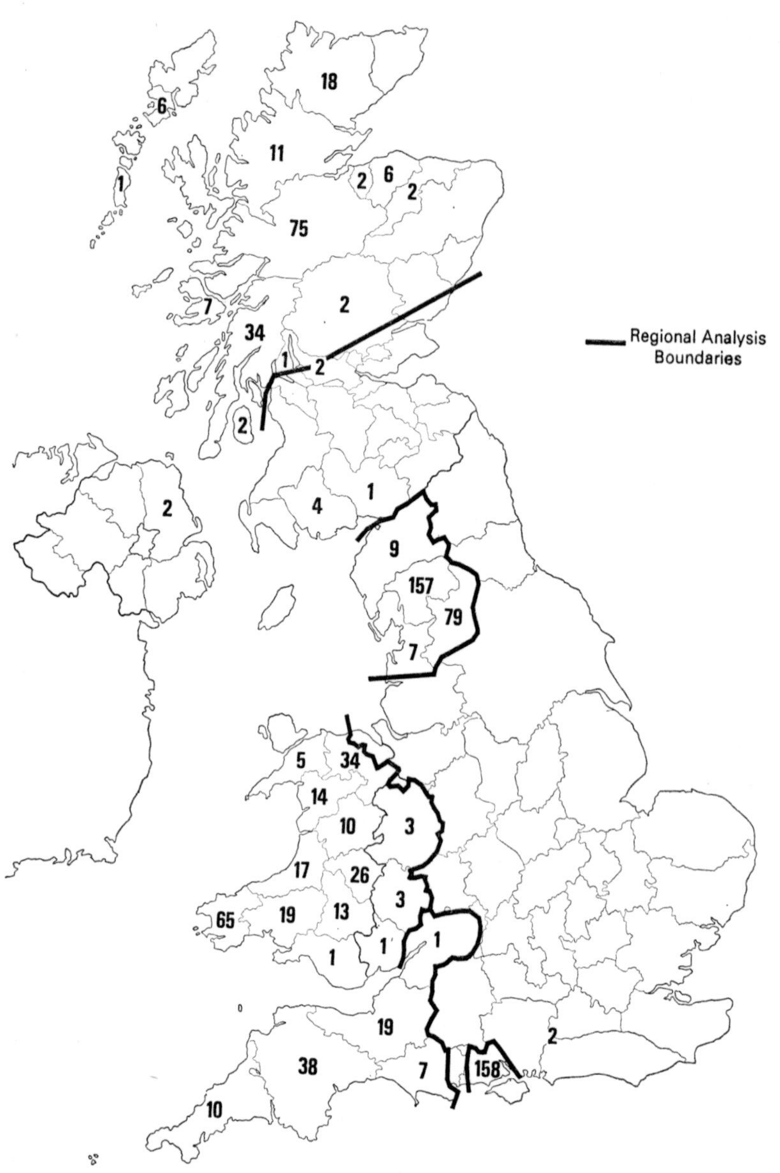

9 Origin of nest record cards for the buzzard, returned to the British Trust for Ornithology, 1937–69

cards returned by counties, there were great geographical disparities in origin. Of the total of 874 cards, 534 or about 60 per cent were from only 5 areas—the New Forest (158 cards); Pembrokeshire (65); Westmorland (157); north-west Yorkshire (79); and Inverness-shire (75). Most of the New Forest cards were filled in by myself in the 1960s. Of the Pembrokeshire cards, 34 were derived from the study of the buzzards of Skomer Island by T. A. W. Davis and D. R. Saunders between 1954 and 1964.[2] The Westmorland and Yorkshire cards extended over the whole 1937–69 period and were returned mainly by the Sedgwick Society of Sedbergh School (whose records have been examined in detail by Michael Holdsworth[3]), R. W. Robson and D. C. Bishop. The cards from Inverness-shire were returned mainly by the Hon Douglas Weir for the years 1964–8.

Table 5 summarises the information obtained from the cards about average clutch size and fledging success for the country as a whole. The number of nests in the clutch size column of the table

TABLE 5

National analysis of clutch size and breeding success of buzzards in Britain, 1937–69

	Clutch size		*Outcome of breeding known*		
Total cards	*No nests*	*Average*	*No cards used*	*Nests failed*	*Average No* young reared*
874	641	2·56	645	146	1·37

* This is the average for *all* nests of known outcome, including total failures.

included some for which this information was inferred from the size of broods (plus remaining eggs, if any) whilst the young were still very small and downy. Addled eggs remain in the nest for some time after the young hatch—they can sometimes be found there, intact, after the young have flown—whilst losses among the chicks are rare in the first week or ten days. The average clutch size given in the table will be minimal in view of the assumptions made, but the margin of error is unlikely to be significant. Similarly, in calculating the average number of young reared, the sample was enlarged by including broods which were fully feathered and almost ready to leave the nest when last seen, but which were not actually proved to have flown. There is no direct relationship in Table 5 (p 155) between the number of clutches whose size was recorded and the number of nests whose outcome was known, because on the one hand many nests found with eggs were not revisited and, on the other, many were found only when they held large young.

Annual averages for clutch size and fledging success for the period 1948–69 (before which the annual sample was very small) are shown in graph form in Fig 10. The main feature of the graph

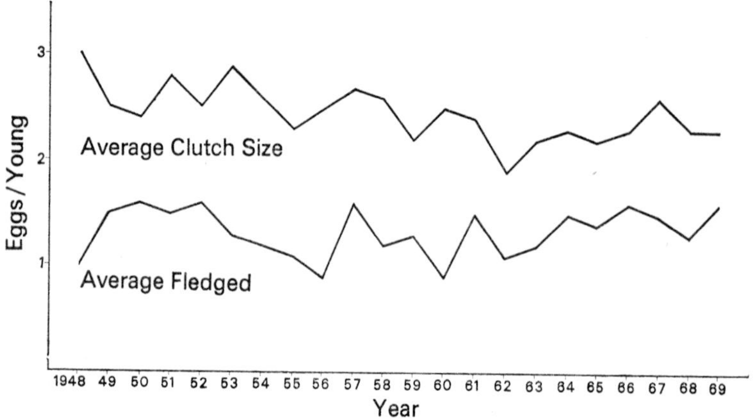

10 National analysis of clutch size and breeding success of buzzards, 1948–69 (from nest record card analysis)

is, perhaps, the relative inconsistency of the figures from year to year, annual average clutch sizes varying between 1·9 and 3·0 eggs, and the average number of young reared per pair between 0·9 and 1·6. A second feature is the slight but progressive decline in average clutch size from 1948 to 1962, and the equally slight increase from 1962 to 1969. Interpretation, however, is hazardous in view of the small size and irregular distribution of the annual sample. Certainly no marked slump in either clutch size or breeding success, such as might be expected to mark the myxomatosis episode after 1954, is readily apparent from Fig 10, though it is true that 1955–6 does coincide with a low point in both curves. Though it is important to remember that the cards give no information about the incidence of non-breeding pairs—which were alleged to be numerous after the onset of myxomatosis—the information derived from them is not inconsistent with the thesis, advanced in Chapter Three, that the impact of myxomatosis on buzzard populations was less severe than has been widely assumed.

The average size of 641 clutches between 1937 and 1969 was 2·56 eggs, and the average number which fledged from the 645 nests for which the outcome was recorded was 1·37 young. For the shorter period 1948–69 with which Fig 10 is concerned, the averages are 2·46 (620 clutches) and 1·33 (625 nests) respectively. Single, addled eggs in otherwise fertile clutches, and losses of one and occasionally two young from broods on the nest were frequent, but the difference between average clutch size and the average number fledged was largely accounted for by the number of complete clutches and broods which failed. Of the 645 nests of known outcome between 1937 and 1969, 146, or about 24 per cent, failed, most of them during the incubation period. These failures are analysed in Table 6, which shows that human predation was the most often recorded cause of losses. Moreover, predation by man is almost certainly under-represented in the table. Only instances in which this was definitely known to be the cause of failure are recorded there, whereas the circumstances in which numerous other clutches and broods disappeared or were deserted, strongly suggested the intervention of man. The implications of the number of clutches found broken were discussed in Chapter Three. Thirty-nine of the 49 clutches and broods recorded as lost to human predation were in north-west England. Only six were in Scotland, three in south-west England and one in the New Forest. Besides

TABLE 6

Clutch and brood losses or buzzards, recorded on nest record cards in Britain, 1937–69

Clutches lost		*Clutches of broods lost*		*Broods lost*	
Circumstances	*No*	*Circumstances*	*No*	*Circumstances*	*No*
Human predation	34	Human predation	8	Human predation	7
Found addled or deserted	32	Disappeared	12	Found dead on nest	7
Found broken	21	Tree blown down	1	Disappeared	7
Disappeared	14	Tree felled	1	Tree felled	1
Nest flooded	1				
Totals	102		22		22

Note: the middle column lists instances in which it was uncertain whether eggs or young had been lost.

losses of eggs and young, a number of cards recorded adult buzzards found shot or trapped at the nest. Gamekeepers, hill farmers and egg collectors are all recorded as taking their toll.

Despite the generally rather dismal reflection of human attitudes towards buzzards to be found in the cards, they did contain some evidence of a relaxation in the persecution of nests since the 1950s—at least in parts of Wales and north-west England, from which about 50 per cent of the failures were reported. Fig 11 shows in graph form the annual percentage of nests which failed during the 1948–69 period, and the percentage which failed due to human persecution. The most conspicuous feature of the graph is the sharp fall in the percentage of failures after 1960, and this is difficult to interpret other than in terms of reduced persecution—which implies, as has already been suggested, that human predation was a more important cause of failure than the actual figures for such losses suggest. It is at least encouraging that in some parts of the uplands there may have been a reduction in human pressures on breeding buzzards in recent years.

In order to explore regional differences, I produced graphs of annual clutch size and fledging success for each of the five regions shown in Fig 9 (p 154), into which the cards naturally fell—the New Forest; south-west England; Wales and the Marches; north-west England; and the Scottish Highlands and Islands. I found, however, that the results could be interpreted only with the greatest caution because of the small and fluctuating size of the annual sample. The only region for which any definite trend was discernible was the Highlands and Islands, where average clutch size showed a sustained rise from 2·0 eggs in 1962 to 3·1 eggs in 1969, and the average number which fledged increased from 1·0

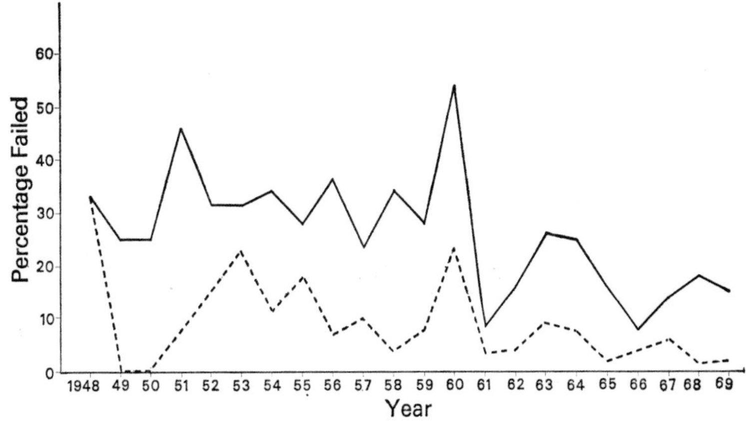

11 Percentage of buzzard nests which failed, 1948–69 (from nest record card analysis)

young to 2·8 young over the same period. For most regions there was a suggestion of larger clutches before the mid-1950s, which would not be inconsistent with the reported effects of myxomatosis, though the number of cards involved was too small to allow firm conclusions.

The most interesting feature to emerge from the comparison of regional data was a latitudinal increase in clutch size and breeding success from south to north. This is illustrated in Table 7, which gives averages for the period 1948–69, before which the data were mainly only from north-west England; and also for 1963–9, because information about clutch sizes in the New Forest before 1963 was inadequate. Larger differences were found between average clutch size and average fledging success in Wales, north-west England and Scotland than in the South—the result of higher predation, mainly human—and in order to show regional differences in potential reproduction more clearly, Table 7 also shows the average number of young fledged from successful nests alone. The table confirms that both clutch size and fledging success

TABLE 7

Average clutch size and fledging success of buzzards in Britain, 1948–69 (from nest record card analysis)

Region	*Average clutch size*		*Average fledged/nest**		*Average fledged/successful nest*	
	1948–69	*1963–9*	*1948–69*	*1963–9*	*1948–69*	*1963–9*
New Forest		1·9		1·2		1·4
South-west England	2·2	2·2	1·2	1·6	1·7	1·9
Wales & the Marches	2·3	2·2	1·2	1·5	1·7	1·9
North-west England	2·5	2·3	1·3	1·5	1·9	1·9
Scottish Highlands	2·7	2·7	1·5	1·9	2·2	2·2

* ie total number of nests the outcome of which was known

in the New Forest from 1963 to 1969 was significantly lower than elsewhere, and that both were highest in the Scottish Highlands. To summarise regional differences more subjectively: in north-west England and the Highlands, over the 1948–69 period, clutches of two or—more often—three eggs were usual, with clutches of four eggs occurring frequently (especially in the Highlands), whilst a clutch of five eggs was recorded from the West Riding of Yorkshire in 1961: single eggs were rare. In Wales and the South-west Peninsula, clutches of two or three eggs were usual, each occurring with approximately equal frequency, whilst clutches of either four or one occurred only occasionally. In the New Forest (between 1963 and 1969) clutches of one or two eggs were normal, with clutches of three eggs occurring less frequently.

To summarise some of the main points of the nest record card analysis, the average size of 641 clutches between 1937 and 1969 was 2·56 eggs, and the average number of young reared from 645 nests whose outcome was known, was 1·37. These 645 nests included 146 which failed completely, mainly during incubation, and largely due to persecution by man. Analysis of the data for different regions, however, suggested a latitudinal increase in clutch size and breeding success from south to north and, in particular, confirmed my earlier impression that both were significantly lower in the New Forest than elsewhere.

How do these results compare with continental data? Clutch size, and to a somewhat lesser extent brood survival, have absorbed many continental ornithologists. In his comprehensive study of the buzzard in Denmark, V. Holstein recorded a mean clutch size of 2·67 eggs, with an average of 2·0 young flying from successful nests.[4] Further south, in north-west Germany, Klaus Warncke and Jochen Wittenberg recorded a mean clutch size of 2·4 eggs. Their main interest, however, was in population density, and they give no information about brood size.[5] T. Mebs also gives a mean of 2·4 for a sample of 298 German clutches, with a mean brood size of 1·9 for successful nests.[6] Many continental buzzard populations, however, exhibit comparatively dramatic variations in clutch size and output of young which are usually described as being associated with the relative abundance of small rodents, though Holstein also claimed a correlation between hard winters, when food was scarce or difficult to obtain, and breeding seasons in which there was a high incidence of non-breeding, addled eggs, and small clutches. Mebs gave an average clutch size of 1·96 eggs for years when voles were few, and 2·85 for years when voles were especially abundant. Victor Wendland, working in the Berlin area between 1940 and 1951, similarly associated increases in output of young with *Feldmausjahren* in a population of buzzards which seem to have had a generally low rate or reproduction compared with other north European populations, only 165 young being produced in 170 pair/years—a lower average than in the New Forest buzzard population.[7]

Clutch size and fledging success are most likely to be related mainly to the amount of prey available. Regionally, average clutch sizes have probably evolved to relate broadly to the largest number of young for which the parent birds can, in an average year, find food. An increase in average clutch size from south to north in the Northern Hemisphere has been noticed in many species of land birds, and it seems not unreasonable to suppose that this phenomenon, which is so evident in the analysis of the nest record cards for the buzzard in Britain, is associated with the increase in potential feeding time made possible by increasing day length. For the buzzard in Britain, this overall trend masks various local variations in average clutch size and fledging success which can reasonably be related to local variations in prey resources.

The buzzard population on the edge of Dartmoor, which Peter Dare studied in 1956–8, was then producing significantly fewer young than the average for south-west England recorded in the nest record card analysis, though average clutch sizes were, in fact, somewhat larger. In the three years, there were respectively 12, 14, and 14 pairs of buzzards in the study area, giving a total of 40 'pair/years'. In only 29 pair/years were eggs laid. Thus, no less than 27 per cent of the population failed to breed at all. The average of 14 clutches whose size was definitely known was 2·43 eggs. In the 29 pair/years in which breeding was attempted, however, only 18 young were reared—0·45 young/pair; or 0·6 young/pair which attempted to breed; or 1·3 young/successful nest. About 40 per cent of the eggs laid did not hatch (6 complete clutches were lost to crows) and there were numerous losses of young birds during the fledgling period. The rabbit population of Dare's study area had recently been hard hit by myxomatosis, and the buzzard population was evidently in the process of adjusting to a smaller available prey-biomass (made up mainly of voles, birds, rabbits and reptiles) under fairly high density conditions—1·0–1·2 pairs/square mile. This seems likely to have accounted for the low output of young, though it is interesting that (in the birds which laid eggs) there was no swift adjustment of clutch size. That conditions had become unstable for buzzards is further suggested by the turnover in the adult population of the study area: excluding the young birds reared in the area, no less than 60–70 different individuals were recognised during the three years.[8]

Speyside, into which buzzards have spread comparatively recently, and which is rich in prey resources, especially rabbits, offers an extreme contrast with Peter Dare's Dartmoor study area. During 1964–71 the Speyside buzzard population was characterised by large clutches of eggs, and very low losses of either eggs or fledglings. Average clutch size was 2·9 eggs, and the average number of young fledged/successful nest was 2·5. Both figures are higher than those derived from all nest record cards (including those from Speyside) for the Scottish Highlands as a whole (see Table 7, p 160). In 1971 the average clutch size in Speyside was as high as 3·2 eggs, and the average brood size was 2·8 young. The density of buzzards in Speyside in 1964–71 was below that of Dare's Dartmoor study area in 1956–8, but despite this and the abundance of prey a proportion (probably about 15 per cent in 1970) of territory-holding buzzards evidently failed to breed in any one year.[9]

The buzzard country in north-west England provides a further contrast. Here, on the sheepwalk of the open fells, the buzzard has evidently arrived at a quite different balance with its prey (mainly short-tailed voles since myxomatosis). Clutch sizes and numbers fledged are relatively high, but to achieve this, territories are many times larger than in Dartmoor or Speyside. The nest record cards yielded an average clutch size of 2·5 eggs for 1948–69, with an average of 1·9 young flying from each successful nest. Clearly, however, there is local variation, and in the area within ten miles of Sedbergh, Michael Holdsworth recorded an average clutch size of 3·03 eggs, and an average brood size of 2·2 young for successful nests between 1937 and 1967. He was also able to demonstrate that the annual output of young varied somewhat with the relative abundance of voles.[10] The Lakeland buzzards (as was mentioned in

Chapter Three) seem to have been less successful, particularly since the 1950s, and though there is some reason to associate this with the use of dieldrin in sheep-dips, it is not clear why buzzards in the ecologically similar country around Sedbergh were apparently not similarly affected.

A further variation in the relationship between food supply, territory size, and output of young appears to be represented in localities which support especially high densities of buzzards. Skomer Island, off the Pembrokeshire coast, is an example. In 1954, at the start of an eleven-year study period, T. A. W. Davis and D. R. Saunders recorded 8 pairs of buzzards on the island's 722 acres, a density presumably made possible by the exceptional numbers of rabbits. Although the buzzard population fell after myxomatosis it remained at 4–5 pairs for the remainder of the study period and, indeed, remains about the same today. Rabbits (despite periodic reductions by myxomatosis) and seabirds, besides Skomer voles, provided abundant food. Despite the abundance of prey, the output of young buzzards was low, even before myxomatosis—it was only 1·37 young/pair in 1954. In 51 pair/years recorded by Davis and Saunders, only 44 young were reared—0·86 per territory-holding pair; or 1·1 per pair which attempted to breed; or 1·7 per pair which bred successfully. These success rates are somewhat lower than the average for Wales derived from the nest record card analysis. The average of 20 clutches whose size was definitely known, however, was somewhat higher than the average from Welsh nest record cards, at 2·6 eggs.[11]

Ramsey Island, nine miles across St Bride's Bay from Skomer, also holds a high-density buzzard population, associated with a superabundance of rabbits. Ramsey is about the same size as Skomer, and in 1972 it held 5 pairs of buzzards, 2 with broods of 1 young, and 3 with broods of 2 young—an average of 1·6 young per pair.[12] Rabbits swarmed on the island, and on the face of it there seemed no reason why all five pairs of buzzards should not easily have found food for broods of three or even four young. It seems, however, that abundance of prey ceases to influence reproductive success once the population has passed a certain threshold of density. Conceptually this is not unreasonable, and it is possible that the buzzard's territorial behaviour provides the mechanism by which adjustment of brood size is achieved, the close proximity of a number of pairs constantly stimulating territorial advertisement and assertion—thus limiting the amount of time available for hunting and, in turn, limiting the buzzard's capacity for rearing large broods. This, however, is largely speculation which it would be of considerable interest to test by careful field study.

The New Forest buzzard population which I studied during 1962–71, exhibited peculiar characteristics which suggested that breeding activity had long been adjusted to a relatively poor prey situation. The population and breeding data for the study period is collected in Table 8, which confirms and amplifies the figures from the nest record card analysis.[13] It will be seen from the table that the population of territory-holding adults remained more or less static—it is doubtful whether the slight increase towards the end of the study period can be considered significant—and that information about breeding (or failure to breed) was obtained for between half and three-quarters of the population each year. In addition to pairs in established territories, it was generally possible to find a few 'singles' during the breeding season, and these, too, would normally set up definite territories (see Chapter Four). In the extensive undulating tracts of woodland in the New Forest, finding buzzards' nests is much more difficult and time consuming than in districts where the woodland is more fragmented, or where the topography is more varied and offers more vantage points from which to watch. To establish what happened to more than 50 per cent of the territory-holding buzzards in the New Forest in any one year was no mean achievement.

In the sense that it was never possible to determine the success of every pair of buzzards, the study area was perhaps too large. It would have been especially valuable to have obtained more definite information about the number of non-breeding pairs each year. Absolute proof of non-breeding is difficult to obtain in most birds of prey, and in dense and extensive woodland the problems are multiplied. Even after prolonged observation and repeated searches of the birds' territory one can comparatively seldom be absolutely convinced that a pair have not attempted to breed in a nest which has been missed. In fact, in the New Forest, an enormous amount of time was spent in search and observation of territories suspected of holding non-breeding pairs, and remembering, particularly, the ease with which nests can often be found late in the season when the young are near the flying stage and are very noisy, the balance of probability is for most years in favour of a greater frequency of non-breeding than is actually recorded in Table 8. The figures for 1966 and 1967, which show that 18–25 per cent failed to breed, probably represent a more or less accurate picture because in both years determined efforts were made to establish the number of non-breeding pairs. Sufficient time was never subsequently available to repeat this, but in my opinion a non-breeding population of between 15 and 25 per cent is probably normal in the New Forest.

Bearing this in mind, the data in Table 8 permit the following main conclusions to be drawn. First, there was a relatively high frequency of non-breeding (say, 20 per cent) and addled or broken clutches (14 per cent allowing for the non-breeding population, or 17 per cent of the pairs for which attempted breeding was recorded), though the figures are not as high as in Peter Dare's Dartmoor population. The phenomenon of egg-breaking has been discussed in Chapter Two. There was no proof that adult buzzards were responsible for the breakages in the forest, and carrion crows were the most likely culprits, but the possibility of some more fundamental environmental reason for breakages should not be completely discarded.

Second, as has already been observed, average clutch size and fledging success was consistently low, the former varying between 1·5 and 2·3 eggs, and the latter between 0·8 and 1·5 young per pair which attempted to breed or between 1·1 and 1·9 young per successful breeding pair. Allowing for about 20 per cent non-breeding, the average number of young reared becomes about one per pair of adults in the population as a whole. In other words, at the end of the summer there are probably half the number of young

TABLE 8

Population and breeding success of buzzards in the New Forest, Hampshire, 1962–71

Year	No of pairs holding territories	Breeding or attempted breeding proved							Pairs failed to lay eggs
		Pairs	Clutches failed to hatch or broken	Average clutch size (No clutches/ average)	Young reared	Average young reared/ nest	Average young reared/ successful nest		
1962	32[1]	16	0	—	20	1·3	1·3		2
1963	34	17	1	11/2·3	24	1·4	1·5		1
1964	33	16	4	9/1·5	13	0·8	1·1		4
1965	33	20	3	13/1·8	25	1·3	1·5		4
1966	33	16	1	7/1·8[2]	24	1·5	1·6		8
1967	33	13	1	1/2·0	14	1·1	1·2		6
1968	33	19	4	12/1·8	20	1·0	1·3		2
1969	36	21	5	9/2·3	30	1·4	1·9		4
1970	36	18	4	2/2·0	23	1·3	1·6		2
1971	37	22	5	5/2·0	27	1·2	1·7		4
TOTAL/ AVERAGE	340	178	28	69/1·86	220	1·23	1·47		37

[1] Three territories occupied 1963 and subsequently were not investigated in 1962.

[2] Includes five nests first inspected when young were very small in which brood size was assumed to equal clutch size.

birds as adults in the study area. Of the 69 clutches whose size was definitely known, 47 were of 2 eggs, 13 were of 1 egg, and 10 were of 3 eggs. Only 4 broods of 3 young were known to have fledged in the study area in 11 years.

Whilst non-breeding or failure to hatch eggs usually occurred intermittently in any one territory, some territories—or their occupants—seemed especially prone to failure. In two instances, pairs failed to rear young in at least six out of eleven years; in three instances they failed in at least four years; and in two instances they failed in at least three years. With one exception these eight territories exhibited no clear ecological differences to more successful territories, the exception (one of those where the birds failed in at least six years) being an area of poorly grown conifer plantation on very acid soils, which was probably faunistically impoverished compared with more typical buzzard territories which include mixed woodland, glades and heath. Despite the absence of any obvious ecological correlation with breeding failure, it seems more likely to be the territory than the birds that possess inherent defects, because breeding failure seldom occurred over more than two consecutive years. This hypothesis could be tested by measuring systematically the relative amounts of prey available in 'good' and 'poor' territories, but the buzzard feeds on such a variety of organisms that this poses considerable difficulties.

The best explanation for the low reproductive rate of the New Forest buzzards lies in a study of their prey. The prey species available in large quantities to the buzzards in the forest are birds of many species, rabbits (which increased steadily during the study, though periodically reduced in any one locality by myxomatosis), reptiles and frogs. Short-tailed voles, which are so important in the diet of buzzards elsewhere (especially on the continent), are far from abundant in the forest. They are essentially associated with grassland, and especially with reasonably long grass, and over most of the forest the relatively limited areas of grassland are eaten bare by the commoners' ponies and cattle. Short-tailed voles thus occur only rather locally, and mostly on agricultural holdings. Wood mice, which are the commonest rodents in the woodland and heathland areas, are mainly nocturnal. Next to wood mice, bank voles are perhaps the most numerous rodent in the forest away from the enclosed, agricultural land and villages; though because of the lack of a regular understory of shrubs in the woods (a result of the forest's long history of intensive grazing) they tend to occur rather locally and are seldom abundant. Some idea of the relative abundance of the different species of small rodents and insectivores may be gained from Table 9, which summarises the results of trapping with Longworth live traps in favourable woodland, woodland edge, and village margin habitats between 1957 and 1961.[14]

TABLE 9

Summary of results from Longworth live trapping in woodland, woodland edge and village margin habitats, New Forest, Hampshire, May 1957–October 1961

Species	*No trap/nights caught*
Wood mouse *Apodemus sylvaticus*	61
Yellow-necked mouse *Apodemus flavicollis*	30
Bank vole *Clethrionomys glareolus*	61
Short-tailed vole *Microtus agrestis*	24
Common shrew *Sorex araneus*	7
Pygmy shrew *Sorex minutus*	2
Water shrew *Neomys fodiens*	2
House mouse *Mus musculus*	2
Total	189
Total trap/nights	582

To round off this brief appraisal of potential food sources, the forest offered numbers of cow and calf carcases in the late winter and early spring. I did not, however, see buzzards taking advantage of this source of carrion—though it supported a wintering pair of ravens between December 1970 and April 1971.

Information about the prey taken by New Forest buzzards was obtained by recording all prey remains found during visits to nests, by analysis of regurgitated pellets, and by noting any identifiable prey that buzzards were seen carrying or delivering to nests. The prey remains found on nests are analysed in Table 10. There are certain limitations to an analysis of this kind, not the least of which is that small rodents or insectivores are usually swallowed whole by well grown young buzzards, and their relics will not often be found on nests. Nevertheless, analysis of 120 pellets confirmed the general picture presented by Table 10. Almost

TABLE 10

*Prey remains recorded from 81 buzzard nests in the New Forest, 1962–70**
Prey is listed in approximate order of frequency of occurrence.

Species	*Frequency of occurrence*
REGULAR	
jackdaw	feathers/remains on 71 nests, often in large quantities
jay	feathers/remains on 50 nests } often collectively in very large quantities
stock dove	feathers/remains on 42 nests }
song thrush	feathers/remains on 29 nests }
woodpigeon	feathers/remains on 21 nests }
rabbit	remains on 3 nests in 1962; no nests in 1963; 1 nest in 1964; and subsequently on practically every nest examined
wood mouse	remains on 31 nests
IRREGULAR	
green woodpecker	8 times on 7 nests (adult remains 5 times, juvenile 3 times)
grey squirrel	8 times on 8 nests
mole	6 times on 6 nests (carcase untouched in each case)
pheasant	remains of chicks 6 times on 5 nests; feathers of adults twice on 2 nests
woodcock	remains of chicks 6 times on 5 nests; feathers of adult once
grass snake	5 times on 4 nests
slow-worm	6 times on 5 nests
magpie	4 times on 4 nests (juvenile once, adult 3 times)
short-tailed vole	5 times on 2 nests
chaffinch	3 times on 3 nests (all adults)
great spotted woodpecker	3 times on 3 nests
tawny owl	twice on 2 nests (juveniles)
hare	twice on 2 nests
carrion crow	twice on 2 nests (juveniles)
CASUAL	
red-legged partridge	once (chick)
meadow pipit	once (juvenile)
white domestic dove	once
starling	once (adult)
robin	once (adult)
redstart	once (nestling)
adder	once
common lizard	once

* Note: no nest interiors were examined during the fledgling period in 1971.

without exception the pellets were composed mainly of feathers (species identified included jackdaw, song thrush, pheasant chick and young woodcock), and rabbit fur and bone. Other items identified were the remains of 12 wood mice, 3 common shrews and 1 mole; a rat skull; an adder; 2 song thrush legs; the claw of a small passerine; and large quantities of beetle remains. The remaining source of information gave 31 sightings of buzzards carrying snakes or slow-worms; 27 sightings of buzzards with bird prey; 19 sightings with rabbits; 17 sightings with small rodents; 6 sightings with lizards; and 5 sightings with frogs. This data is, of course, strongly biased towards the prey which is most easily identifiable at a distance in a buzzard's talons—hence the large number of snakes or slow-worms recorded. It seems clear, however, that small and medium-sized birds, adults as well as young, form the bulk of the buzzard's prey in the New Forest at least during the breeding season, with rabbits, wood mice and, perhaps, reptiles following in order of importance.

On the face of it the main prey species are together sufficiently abundant to provide an adequate prey-biomass for the forest buzzard population. The main deficiencies in prey sources appear to arise from the small and fluctuating size of the rabbit population, and the limited availability—because of its nocturnal habits—of the wood mouse. It would appear that dependence of the buzzard population on avian prey, which must require more time and more skill to catch than rabbits or mice, has failed to make good a deficit in mammalian food. Clutch size—and fledging success—has adjusted accordingly.

An alternative hypothesis which was examined was that dependence on avian prey had exposed the buzzard population to contamination from organochlorine pesticide residues which had in turn affected breeding performance. The results of analysis for organochlorine residues in fifteen addled eggs which I collected from forest buzzard nests between 1963 and 1968 are given in Table 11. No egg was completely free from pesticide residues, although in most cases these were extremely small. Only in three eggs did total residues exceed 3ppm (of egg content without shell).

The eggs collected most recently—in 1966 and 1968—contained only negligible residues. The New Forest is not sheep country, and this is perhaps reflected in the low dieldrin residues recorded, though the comparatively high concentration in the egg from territory 20 is somewhat anomalous. The immediate source of the residues can only have been the buzzards' avian prey. It is possible that jackdaws, in particular, were the source of contamination for pairs of buzzards which 'specialised' in them, for jackdaws nesting in the forest woodlands continue to feed extensively on agricultural land some distance away during the breeding season. The level of contamination found in most of the eggs analysed, however, did not suggest that pesticides were responsible for the low output of young buzzards in the population as a whole, though it is possible that individual adults were adversely affected.

It is of interest to speculate about the antiquity of the present situation in the New Forest. Local hearsay has it that clutches and broods were larger before myxomatosis than since, but opinions expressed long after the event are of doubtful value and definite records are lacking. Moreover, the rabbit never achieved great abundance in the forest and remained confined to rather small and scattered warrens. It remains possible, however, that the present small average clutch and brood sizes of New Forest buzzards date no further back than the mid-1950s.

The number of young buzzards in a population at the end of the breeding season will seldom exceed the number of adults, and in most areas will be considerably smaller. In the New Forest, for example, there are likely to be about half as many young birds as adults in the late summer and early autumn. In Dare's Dartmoor population there were less than a quarter. At the other extreme, at the end of a season in Speyside, there are probably about the same number of young as adults. Most of all of these young buzzards have dispersed from their area of origin by the late autumn. Comparatively few survive to breed.

Douglas Weir and Nick Picozzi have produced some interesting information about the movements of young buzzards in Speyside, and their study is still continuing. Of 41 young buzzards colour-

Organochlorine residues in eggs of buzzards from the New Forest, Hampshire, 1963–8

Analyses were carried out by the Laboratory of the Government Chemist for the Nature Conservancy, using gas-liquid chromotography. Results are expressed in parts per million of entire egg content without the shell. Where the amount of a compound was less than 0·1ppm this is recorded as 'trace': a dash means that none was detected.

Territory no	*Year*	*Eggs collected and breeding data*	*Weight egg content (g)*	*DDE*	*TDE*	*DDT*	*Dieldrin*	*Hepta-chlor epoxide*	*BHC isomers*	*Total residues*
6	1963	1 from c/2; 1 young reared	43·8	0·9	0·5	0·4	1·2	0·2	—	3·2
37	1963	c/2 collected	35·5 43·0	0·6 0·5	0·5 0·4	0·3 0·3	0·3 0·2	— —	— —	1·7 1·4
36	1964	1 from c/2; 1 young reared	43·5	0·2	—	—	0·1	trace	trace	0·3
36	1965	1 from c/2; 1 young reared	38·3	1·0	trace	0·2	0·2	trace	—	1·4
32	1965	1 from addled c/2	37·0	0·7	0·1	—	trace	—	—	0·8
28	1965	1 from c/2; 1 young reared	45·2	0·2	trace	trace	0·2	trace	—	0·4
2	1965	1 from c/2; 1 young reared	42·4	0·3	0·1	0·1	0·3	0·1	—	0·9
23	1965	1 from c/3; 2 young reared	44·5	1·6	0·6	0·3	0·5	trace	—	3·0
20	1965	addled c/1	33·7	0·6	—	0·4	4·4	trace	—	5·4
33	1966	addled c/1	45·0	0·3	—	—	0·3	trace	—	0·6
36	1966	1 from c/2; 1 young reared	48·0	0·2	—	—	0·1	trace	—	0·3
33	1968	addled c/1	43·0	0·2	—	—	trace	—	—	0·2
30	1968	1 from c/2; 1 young reared	47·3	trace	—	—	trace	—	—	trace
6	1968	1 from c/2; 1 young reared	41·4	0·2	—	—	—	—	—	0·2
		MEAN:		0·5	0·15	0·13	0·52	0·02	—	1·32

ringed in the Speyside study area in 1969 only 2 were seen there subsequently, though the legs of at least 40 individual buzzards were inspected in winter 1969–70. Two others were recovered dead: one in the following January 50 miles east, and the other in the following February, 50 miles south-east. One of the colour-ringed birds set up a winter territory in the study area, but a number of other young birds which wintered there were not ringed, and had probably immigrated to the area from elsewhere. All remained within areas of about 100 acres, which they defended against other buzzards and which were distributed between the territories of established pairs.[15]

The best evidence about the movements—and mortality—of young buzzards is derived from the British Trust for Ornithology ringing scheme. More than 1,500 young buzzards have now been ringed as fledglings in Britain, and up to 1971 106 had been recovered, no less than 82 of them before they were a year old. Of these 106 recoveries, 3 were found dead on the nest where they had been ringed; 6 were found in the immediate vicinity of the nest; 38 had travelled less than 10 miles; 21 between 11 and 20 miles; 13 between 21 and 30 miles; 11 between 31 and 40 miles; 1 between 41 and 50 miles; and the remaining 13, more than 50 miles.

A total of 84 young buzzards were ringed in the New Forest between 1957 and 1969 (all between 1962 and 1969 except for a brood of 3 in 1957) of which 7 have so far been recovered. Five of these were recovered between 18 and 35 miles away in various directions, but the remaining 2 covered record distances for British buzzards, and one has the distinction of being the only British ringed buzzard to have been recovered abroad. Both were ringed in the forest in 1962. One was killed in a pole-trap 270 miles ESE at La Malmaison, Aisne, France, on 28 September 1962. The other was found dying 215 miles NNE at Rowlston, Hornsea, Yorkshire, on 17 September 1962. Neither could have left their parents' territory more than about six weeks at the most before they died. The distance travelled by both birds is many times greater than the average for all British buzzards, which is 22 miles.

Thus, most young buzzards disperse widely but only a comparatively short distance from where they fledged. Some individuals may possibly remain close to their parents' territory if space permits. There is, however, no evidence from the ringing recoveries that, having survived their traumatic immaturity, the young buzzards habitually return to their area of origin to be assimilated back into the population there—though one of Douglas Weir and Nick Picozzi's 1969 colour-ringed birds did reappear, briefly, close to its birthplace in 1970.

Over much of its world range the more northerly buzzard populations tend to be migratory. Those in northern Europe and western Asia are strongly so, birds from some areas wintering as far south as Arabia and East Africa.

The migration of the buzzard population of Fenno-Scandia has been studied in detail from ringing returns by Viking Olsson, who had described the massive exodus from Sweden (much of it across the famed point of Falsterbo) which occurs annually between late August and November, the birds moving on south and west to winter mainly in France and the Low Countries. These migratory buzzards evidently return in successive winters to the same area and remain in definite territories. This south- and west-orientated migratory population includes not only birds of the nominate race but also individuals of the *vulpinus* subspecies, the steppe buzzard, though the latter tends to travel further and apparently winters as far south as North Africa.[16] Noel Mayard, in an analysis of about 300 recoveries in France of buzzards ringed elsewhere, recorded 115 recoveries of Swedish and Norwegian birds of the nominate race, and 12 recoveries of *vulpinus*. German and Swiss ringed buzzards moved considerably shorter distances than those from Scandinavia, though there appeared to be a similar orientation in the general direction of movement.[17] There has so far been no recovery in Britain of a buzzard ringed abroad, though the irregular appearance of small numbers down the east coast in August and September does suggest that the south-westerly movement of European birds sometimes reaches this country. The extent of immigration from the continent, however, is probably small, and a buzzard seen in Britain in the autumn and winter is most likely to be one which was bred in this country.

British ringing recoveries suggest that few young buzzards survive their first winter. Most are either reported trapped or shot, or are found under circumstances suggesting that man was responsible for their demise. Eighty-two out of the total of 106—77·6 per cent—were recovered in their first year; 14, or 13·2 per cent, aged 1–2; 5, or 4·7 per cent, aged 2–3; and only 5 more than 3 years old. There is some doubt about whether buzzards are sexually mature in their first or second breeding seasons, but, if the recoveries are accepted as a fair reflection of mortality in the population as a whole, then at least 77 per cent fail to reach breeding age. If, as is more likely, they do not breed until their second season, then, in Britain, more than 90 per cent die before maturity. In the migratory Scandinavian population, Olsson calculated from the ringing recoveries that 56·6 per cent died in their first year and a further 13 per cent in their second year. At least 65 per cent of the recoveries were of birds shot, trapped, 'killed' or 'caught'.

Once it is mature, a buzzard's life expectation increases considerably. Olsson calculated this as 5·38 years for all buzzards more than a year old in the Scandinavian population. In Britain, with an apparently much higher mortality before maturity, the life span of an adult buzzard should theoretically be longer than in the Scandinavian population if a balance is to be maintained between reproduction and mortality. Taking the average brood size from the nest record card analysis, 1·37 young, and allowing for 90 per cent mortality among immature birds, the average life span of a buzzard once it has achieved maturity should be about seven years. It is not inconceivable that British buzzards, once established in a territory, do indeed tend to live longer than Scandinavian buzzards which have to face the hazards of an annual migration. The calculation, however, is based on the very high immature mortality figure of 90 per cent (and on the assumption, of course, of a static adult population), and it is possible that this is biased by a tendency for more immature buzzards to be found after they have died than mature buzzards because the young birds tend to wander into areas where they are more likely to come into contact with man.

Starting from the British ringing recoveries, the life expectation of a buzzard once it has reached its third year can be calculated as 3·5 more years. Assuming, once again, an average brood size of 1·37 young, and allowing for 90 per cent mortality, it will be found that reproduction fails to balance mortality. The recent history of the buzzard in this country does not support any such suggestion and one is driven back to the conclusion that the 90 per cent mortality recorded for young buzzards is suspect because they are more likely to be found than older birds.

It is probable that an adult life of 4–6 years, and a total life span of 6–8 years, is normal for British buzzards which reach maturity, though some individuals clearly live much longer than this. The British ringing recoveries include 2 birds which were respectively 11 and 12 years old, and there are numerous continental recoveries of birds of comparable age. Viking Olsson referred to 2 buzzards that were aged 17 years 8 months and 17 years 6 months when they were (inevitably) shot. I believe the oldest known buzzard was ringed as a youngster on Heligoland on 1 June 1927, and recovered in Mecklenburg on 21 March 1951, when it was no less than 23 years 10½ months old.[18] In the absence of persecution, and once well established in and familiar with a territory well endowed with prey, there seems every likelihood of a buzzard achieving a considerable age. Certainly I feel sure that at least half a dozen individuals in the New Forest have survived the whole span of my study there.

Despite the high rate of immature mortality—due mainly to man—the buzzard has not only survived but has, in the twentieth century, spread back over much of the ground which it lost in the nineteenth. It is thus probable that mortality would be high among young buzzards even if shooting and trapping were to cease altogether—though this is no excuse for the keeper who sets a pole-trap for the young buzzard which has had the temerity to set up a winter territory on his beat. There can be little serious doubt that the activities of gamekeepers are currently resulting in an unnaturally high mortality among immature buzzards, and that if trapping and shooting were to cease buzzards would colonise much of the country from which they are at present excluded. Apart from the legal and moral arguments against the persecution of birds of prey there is a good deal of evidence that under most circumstances they have negligible effects on game-bird populations. The buzzard is particularly innocent in this respect, as the prey analyses referred to in this book will readily confirm.

A well run shoot has, in fact, much to offer wildlife conservation. Good pheasant and partridge habitat is good habitat for other creatures. Many a hedgerow and copse has been reprieved because of its benefit to game. However, as Derek Barber (himself a shooting man) commented in a *New Scientist* article in April 1972, there are two indictments which can fairly be laid against shooting interests.[19] First, the barbaric cruelty of the pole-trap is still too widely tolerated, and second, the recovery of a number of avian predators is still seriously limited by the activities of gamekeepers. In an era of increasing public awareness of the countryside, birds of prey, and especially the comparatively large and spectacular species such as buzzards and harriers, are assuming the stature of visual assets. I should like to believe that many more of those who control the land and rear game will come to view the buzzard and other predators in this light.

APPENDIX

Scientific Names of Species Mentioned in the Text

Adder *Vipera berus*
Alder *Alnus glutinosa*
Ash *Fraxinus excelsior*

Badger *Meles meles*
Bear, brown *Ursus arctos*
Beech *Fagus sylvatica*
Beetle
  dung *Gotrupes* spp
  ground *Carabidae* spp
Birch *Betula* spp
Blackbird *Turdus merula*
Buzzard *Buteo buteo*
Buzzard, honey *Pernis apivorus*

Cat
  domestic *Felis*
  wild *Felis catus*
Chaffinch *Fringilla coelebs*
Chough *Pyrrhocorax pyrrhocorax*
Coot *Fulica atra*
Coypu *Myocastor coypus*
Crow, carrion *Corvus corone*
Cuckoo, *Cuculus canorus*
Curlew *Numenius arquata*

Dipper *Cinclus cinclus*
Dove, stock *Columba oenas*

Eagle
  golden *Aquila chrysaetos*
  sea *Haliaetus albicilla*

Fir, douglas *Pseudotsuga menziesii*
Fox *Vulpes vulpes*
Frog, common *Rana temporaria*

Goshawk *Accipiter gentilis*
Grebe
  great crested *Podiceps cristatus*
  little *Podiceps ruficollis*
Grouse, red *Lagopus lagopus*
Gull, black-headed *Larus ridibundus*

Hare *Lepus* spp
Harrier
  hen *Circus cyaneus*
  marsh *Circus aeruginosus*
Hawk, red-tailed *Buteo jamaicensis*
Hawthorn, *Crataegus monogyna*
Hazel *Corylus avellana*
Hedgehog *Erinaceus europaeus*
Heron, grey *Ardea cinerea*
Hobby *Falco subbuteo*
Holly *Ilex aquifolium*

Ivy *Hedera helix*

Jackdaw *Corvus monedula*
Jay *Garrulus glandarius*

Kestrel *Falco tinnunculus*
Kingfisher *Alcedo atthis*
Kite, red *Milvus milvus*

Larch *Larix* spp
Leather-jacket grubs *Tipulid* spp
Lizard, common *Lacerta vivipara*

Magpie *Pica pica*
Marten, pine *Martes martes*
Merlin *Falco columbarius*
Mole *Talpa europaea*
Moorhen *Gallinula chloropus*
Mouse
  house *Mus musculus*
  wood *Apodemus sylvaticus*
  yellow-necked *Apodemus flavicollis*

Oak *Quercus* spp
Osprey *Pandion haliaetus*
Otter *Lutra lutra*
Owl
  barn *Tyto alba*
  little *Athene noctua*
  short-eared *Asio flammeus*
  tawny *Strix aluco*

Partridge *Perdix perdix*
  red-legged *Alectoris rufa*
Penguin, Adelie *Pygoscelis adeliae*
Peregrine *Falco peregrinus*
Pheasant *Phasianus colchicus*
Pigeon, wood *Columba palumbus*
Pine
  Corsican *Pinus laricio*
  Scots *Pinus sylvestris*
  Weymouth *Pinus strobus*
Pipit, meadow *Anthus trivialis*
Polecat *Putorius putorius*
Puffin *Fratercula arctica*
Purple moor-grass *Molinia caerulea*

Rabbit *Oryctolagus cuniculus*
Rat, brown *Rattus norvegicus*
Raven *Corvus corax*
Redshank *Tringa totanus*
Redstart *Phoenicurus phoenicurus*
Reindeer *Rangifer tarandus*

Robin *Erithacus rubecula*
Rook *Corvus frugilegus*

Shrew *Sorex* spp
Shrew
  common *Sorex araneus*
  pygmy *Sorex minutus*
  water *Neomys fodiens*
Skua *Stercorarius* spp
Skylark *Alauda arvensis*
Slow-worm *Anguis fragilis*
Snake, grass *Natrix natrix*
Snipe *Gallinago gallinago*
Sparrow, house *Passer domesticus*
Sparrowhawk *Accipiter nisus*
Spruce *Picea* spp
Squirrel
  grey *Neosciurus carolinensis*
  red *Sciurus vulgaris*
Starling *Sternus vulgaris*
Stoat *Mustula erminea*

Thrush, song *Turdus philomelos*

Vole
  bank *Clethrionomys glareolus*
  common *Microtus arvalis*
  short-tailed *Microtus agrestis*
  Skomer *Clethrionomys glareolus skomerensis*
  water *Arvicola amphibius*

Weasel *Mustula nivalis*
Wolf *Canis lupus*
Woodcock *Scolopax rusticola*
Woodpecker
  great spotted *Dendrocopos major*
  green *Picus viridis*

Yellowhammer *Emberiza citrinella*

NOTES AND REFERENCES

Chapter One *The Buzzard* (pages 15–35)

1 Saunders, Howard. *Manual of British Birds* (1889)

2 Wise, J. R. *The New Forest, Its History and Scenery* (1863)

3 Notably Hartert, Ernst. 'Types of Birds in the Tring Museum', *Novitates Zool*, 27 (1925), 259–76

4 Vaurie, Charles. 'Systematic Notes on Palearctic Birds. No 47 Accipitridae: The Genus *Buteo*', *American Museum Novitates*, 2042 (1961)

5 eg Swann, H. Kirke. *A Monograph of the Birds of Prey*, 1 (1926), 277–396

6 See Vaurie, loc cit

7 Moore, N. W. 'The Past and Present Status of the Buzzard in the British Isles', *Brit Birds*, 50 (1957), 173–97

8 Prestt, Ian. 'An Enquiry into the Recent Breeding Status of some of the Smaller Birds of Prey and Crows in Britain', *Bird Study*, 12 (1965), 196–221

9 See Moore, loc cit

10 Davis, T. A. W. and Saunders, D. R. 'Buzzards on Skomer Island, 1954–64', *Nature in Wales*, 9 (1965), 116–24

11 Weir, D. N. and Picozzi, N. 'Work on Buzzards', in *Research on Vertebrate Predators in Scotland*, The Nature Conservancy (Edinburgh, 1970)

12 Hurrell, H. G. 'Census of Buzzards, 1929', *Devon Birds*, 5 (1952), 34–7

13 Moore, Robert. *The Birds of Devon*, Newton Abbot (1969)

14 Everett, M. J. 'The Golden Eagle Survey in Scotland in 1964–8', *Brit Birds*, 64 (1971), 49–56

15 Gause, G. F. *The Struggle for Existence*, Baltimore (1934)
16 See eg Blondel, Jacques. 'Réflexions sur les rapports entre predateurs et proies chez les rapaces—I. Les effets de la predation sur les populations de proies', *La Terre et la Vie*, 21 (1967), 5–62
17 Davis and Saunders, loc cit
18 Tubbs, C. R. 'Population Study of Buzzards in the New Forest during 1962–6', *Brit Birds*, 60 (1967), 381–95
19 Dare, P. J. *Ecological Observations on a Breeding Population of Common Buzzards* Buteo buteo *(L.) with Particular Reference to the Diet and Feeding Habits*, PHD thesis, unpublished, Exeter University (1961)
20 MacNally, L. 'Food at a Buzzard's Nest', *Scottish Birds*, 2 (1962), 196–8
21 Harting, J. E. *A Handbook of British Birds* (1901)
22 Morris, F. O. *A History of British Birds*, I (1903)
23 Czarnecki, Zygamunt, and Foksowicz, Tadeusz. 'Observations on the Composition of the Food of the Buzzard', *Ecologia Polska* (1954), 477–84
24 See eg Bergman, Goran. 'The Food of Birds of Prey and Owls in Fenno-Scandia', *Brit Birds*, 54 (1961), 308–9; Melde, M. *Der Mäusebussard*, Wittenberg Lutherstadt (1956); Zharkov, N. V. and Teplov, A. V. 'Food of the Predatory Birds of the Tatarian Republic', *Roboty Volsko-Kamsko Zonal Ocht Promysl Biol St*, 7–8 (1932), 138–99; Toufar, J. 'Zur Kenntnis der Nahrung Nestjunger Mäusebussard', *Sylvia*, 15 (1958), 67–76
25 Pinowski, Jan and Ryszkowski, Lech 'The Buzzard's Versatility as a Predator', *Brit Birds*, 55 (1962), 470–5
26 Thiollay, Jean-Marc. 'Ecologie d'une population de rapaces diurnes en Lorraine', *La Terre et la Vie*, 2 (1967), 116–95
27 See Harting, op cit
28 Hayman, R. W. 'Persistent Ground-feeding by Buzzards', *Brit Birds*, 63 (1970), 133
29 Pinowski and Ryszkowski, loc cit
30 The predator–prey relationship is a complex subject. For useful summaries see Blondel, loc cit, and the companion paper by: Frochot, B. 'Réflexions sur les rapports entre predateurs et proies chez les rapaces—II. L'influence des proies sur les rapaces', *La Terre et la Vie*, 21 (1967), 29–58; and Murton, R. K. *Man and Birds* (1971)
31 Snow, D. W. 'Movements and Mortality of British Kestrels', *Bird Study*, 15 (1968), 65–83

32 Southern, H. N. 'The Natural Control of a Population of Tawny Owls *Strix aluco*', *J Zool Lond*, 162 (1970), 197–285
33 Holdsworth, Michael, 'Breeding Biology of Buzzards at Sedbergh during 1937–67', *Brit Birds*, 64 (1971), 412–20
34 See eg Mellanby, Kenneth. *Pesticides and Pollution* (1967)
35 See esp Ratcliffe, D. A. 'Changes Attributable to Pesticides in Egg Breakage Frequency and Eggshell Thickness in some British Birds', *J Appl Ecol*, 7 (1970), 67–115

Chapter Two *Decline : c1600–1914* (pages 36–61)

1 Harting, J. E. *British Mammals Extinct within Historic Times* (1880)
2 Cox, J. C. *The Royal Forests of England* (1905)
3 Turner, William. *Avium Praecipuarum*, Cologne (1544)
4 Willughby, Francis and Ray, John. *Ornithologia*, II (1678)
5 Pennant, Thomas. *British Zoology*, II (1776)
6 Latham, John. *A General Synopsis of Birds*, I (1781)
7 For a succinct account of the social and economic changes taking place see: Tate, W. E. *The English Village Community and the Enclosure Movements* (1967)
8 Cox, J. C. *Churchwardens' Accounts, from the late fourteenth century to the close of the seventeenth century* (1913)
9 Hampshire Record Office, 32M69/12
10 Cox, op cit
11 Sheail, John. *Rabbits and their History*, Newton Abbot (1971)
12 Borrer, William. *The Birds of Sussex* (1891)
13 D'Urban, W. S. M. and Mathew, M. A. *The Birds of Devon* (1895)
14 Macpherson, H. A. and Duckworth, W. *The Birds of Cumberland*, Carlisle (1886)
15 Ticehurst, N. F. 'Rewards for Vermin-killing paid by the Churchwardens of Tenterden, 1626 to 1712', *Hastings and East Sussex Naturalist*, 5 (1935), 69–82; Ticehurst, N. F. 'On the Former Abundance of the Kite, Buzzard and Raven in Kent', *Brit Birds*, 14 (1920), 34–7
16 An extensive collection of Hampshire churchwardens' accounts is held in the Hampshire County and Diocesan Record Office. See also: Williams, J. F. (ed). *The Early Churchwardens' Accounts of Hampshire*, Winchester (1913), which gives transcripts of all extant accounts before 1600.

17 Cox, op cit, 1913; Blundell, M. (ed). *Blundell's Diary and Letter Book 1702–28*, Liverpool (1952); Rollinson, W. *A History of Man in the Lake District* (1967), fn 130

18 Hampshire Record Office, 39M68/13

19 See eg Elliott, J. S. *Bedfordshire Vermin Payments*, Luton (1936), which gives breakdowns of the vermin kill by species and parish, mainly for the eighteenth and nineteenth centuries.

20 There are many descriptions of sparrow-catching drives, though mostly for the nineteenth century. See eg Robinson, M. *A South Down Farm in the Sixties* (1938); Knight, S. *A Cotswold Lad* (1960)

21 The allusions here to the process of enclosure necessarily contain elements of over-simplification: see Tate, op cit

22 For an account of the changes in the landscape arising from enclosure see: Hoskins, W. G. *The Making of the English Landscape* (1969 edn)

23 Dixon, Charles. *Lost and Vanishing Birds* (1898)

24 Lilford, Lord. *Notes on the Birds of Northamptonshire*, I (1880–3)

25 St John, Charles. *A Tour in Sutherlandshire*, Edinburgh (1884), 177

26 Wise, John R. *The New Forest, its History and Scenery* (1863), 275–6

27 More, A. G. 'On the Distribution of Birds in Great Britain during the Nesting Season', *Ibis*, New Series, 1, January 1865. This summarised information received from what amounts to a questionnaire circulated to correspondents throughout the country.

28 The data in Table 1 are derived mainly from James Ritchie's classic pioneer study in ecological history, *The Influence of Man on Animal Life in Scotland: A Study in Faunal Evolution*, Cambridge (1920); they were tabulated with two minor errors and the addition of the Glengarry material by Professor W. H. Pearsall, *Mountains and Moorlands* (1950)

29 Ibid

30 More, loc cit, 12

31 Moore, N. W. 'The Past and Present Status of the Buzzard in the British Isles', *Brit Birds*, 50 (1957), 173–97

32 Ticehurst, C. B. *A History of the Birds of Suffolk* (1932)

33 Blaythwayt, F. L. *The Birds of Lincolnshire*, Louth (1914)

34 Walpole-Bond, J. *A History of Sussex Birds*, II (1938)

35 eg Kelsall, J. E. and Munn, P. W. *The Birds of Hampshire and the Isle of Wight* (1905), record nests in 1886 and 1887 in Doles Wood, near Andover—from the second of which, W. H. Turle stole two eggs.

36 Harvie-Browne, J. A. and Buckley, V. F. *A Vertebrate Fauna of the Moray Basin*, Edinburgh (1895); Baxter, E. V. and Rintoul, L. J. *The Birds of Scotland* (1953)
37 Thompson, William. *The Natural History of Ireland* (1849)
38 Watters, John J. *The Natural History of the Birds of Ireland*, Dublin (1853)
39 Usher, Richard and Warren, Robert. *The Birds of Ireland* (1900); Kennedy, P. G., Ruttledge, R. F. and Scroope, C. F. *The Birds of Ireland* (1954)
40 Mathew, M. A. *The Birds of Pembrokeshire* (1894)
41 Mitchell, F. S. *The Birds of Lancashire* (1892); Macpherson, H. A. and Duckworth, W. *The Birds of Cumberland*, Carlisle (1886); Nelson, T. H. *The Birds of Yorkshire* (1906); Macpherson, H. A. *A Vertebrate Fauna of Lakeland*, Edinburgh (1892); and the relevant *Victoria County Histories*
42 Baxter and Rintoul, op cit
43 Harvie-Browne, J. A. and Buckley, V. F. *A Vertebrate Fauna of Sutherland, Caithness and Western Cromarty*, Edinburgh (1887)
44 Harvie-Browne, J. A. and Macpherson, H. A. *A Vertebrate Fauna of the North-West Highlands and Skye*, Edinburgh (1904)
45 Wise, John, op cit, 307
46 Lascelles, Hon G. W. *Thirty-Five Years in the New Forest* (1915), 56, 58
47 Meinertzhagen, R. *The Diary of a Black Sheep* (1964), 303

Chapter Three *Recovery: 1915–71* (pages 62–91)

1 Morris, Sir Daniel (ed). *A Natural History of Bournemouth and District*, Bournemouth Natural Science Society (1914), 287
2 Jourdain, F. C. R. 'The Birds of the Oxford District', in Walker, J. J. (ed). *The Natural History of the Oxford District* (1926), 131
3 Annual ornithological reports, *Wiltshire Archaeological Magazine*
4 Blaythwayt, F. L. 'A Revised List of the Birds of Dorset', *Proc Dorset Nat Hist and Arch Soc* (1945), 108
5 Palmer, M. and Ballance, D. K. *The Birds of Somerset* (1968)
6 Hurrell, H. G. 'Census of Buzzards 1929', *Devon Birds*, 5 (3), (Oct 1952), 34–7. (Reprint of report first published in *The Western Morning News* for 28 August 1929)
7 See eg Bolan, G. *The Birds of Northumberland*, Newcastle (1932);

Chislett, Ralph. *Yorkshire Birds* (1960); Oakes, Clifford. *The Birds of Lancashire* (1953)

8 Baxter, E. V. and Rintoul, L. J. *The Birds of Scotland* (1953)

9 Ruttledge, R. F. *Ireland's Birds* (1966). See also: Kennedy, P. G., Ruttledge, R. F. and Scroope, C. F. *The Birds of Ireland* (1954)

10 Moore, N. W. 'The Past and Present Status of the Buzzard in the British Isles', *Brit Birds*, 50 (1957), 173–97

11 Lord, J. and Munns, D. J. *Atlas of Breeding Birds of the West Midlands*, West Midland Bird Club (1970)

12 Des Forges, G. and Harber, D. D. *The Sussex Bird Report* (1954), 11

13 Oakes, Clifford, op cit

14 Bell, T. H. *The Birds of Cheshire*, Altrincham (1962)

15 Adcock, Reginald. 'Success Crowns a Buzzard Experiment', *The Field* (13 September 1941), 333

16 Blaythwayt, F. L. 'Reports on Dorset Birds', *Proc Dorset Nat Hist and Arch Soc* (1947 et seq)

17 Annual Reports on Wiltshire Birds, *Wiltshire Archaeological Magazine* (1946 et seq)

18 Annual Reports on Hampshire Birds, *Proc Hampshire Field Club and Arch Soc* (1946 et seq)

19 Cohen, Edwin. *The Birds of Hampshire and the Isle of Wight* (1963)

20 At present in the possession of the writer

21 Peter Day was an acute observer who knew the forest well. His MS notes were examined by kind permission of his nephew, Mr Michael Day.

22 Moore, loc cit (1957), 182

23 Davis, T. A. W. and Saunders, D. R. 'Buzzards on Skomer Island', 1954–64', *Nature in Wales*, 9 (1965), 116–24

24 Lockley, R. M. *The Birds of Pembrokeshire*, West Wales Field Society (1949); Mathew, M. A. *The Birds of Pembrokeshire* (1894)

25 Ruttledge, op cit

26 Willughby, Francis. *Ornithologia*, II (1676)

27 The history of rabbit populations in Britain in this and the previous paragraph is necessarily a crude outline and reference should be made to: Sheail, John. *Rabbits and their History*, Newton Abbot (1971), for a definitive account

28 Ibid

29 Moore, loc cit (1957). See also: Moore, N. W. 'Rabbits, Buzzards and

Hares. Two Studies on the Indirect Effects of Myxomatosis', *La Terre et la Vie*, 103 (1956), 220–5

30 See map showing the distribution of rabbits before myxomatosis, in: Thompson, H. V. and Worden, A. N. *The Rabbit* (1956): this was reproduced in Sheail, op cit, 203

31 Dare, Peter. 'The post-Myxomatosis Diet of the Buzzard', *Devon Birds*, X (Feb 1957), 2–6

32 Manning, C. G. in *Devon Birds*, X (Feb 1957), 7

33 Davis and Saunders, loc cit

34 Ash, J. S. 'Bird of Prey Numbers on a Hampshire Game Preserve during 1952–9', *Brit Birds*, 53 (1960), 285–300

35 Des Forges, C. G. and Harber, D. D. *A Guide to the Birds of Sussex* (1963)

36 Holdsworth, Michael. 'Breeding Biology of Buzzards at Sedbergh during 1937–67', *Brit Birds*, 64 (1971), 412–20

37 Heathcote, A. (ed). *The Birds of Glamorgan*, Cardiff Naturalists Society (1967)

38 Sheail, op cit

39 Moore, loc cit

40 Holdsworth, loc cit

41 Prestt, Ian. 'An Enquiry into the Recent Breeding Status of some of the Smaller Birds of Prey and Crows in Britain', *Bird Study*, 12 (1965), 196–221

42 Ratcliffe, D. A. 'Organochlorine Residues in some Raptor and Corvid Eggs from Northern Britain', *Brit Birds* 58 (1965), 65–81

43 Robson, R. W., in litt, 18 October 1970

44 George, J. L. and Frear, D. E. H. 'Pesticides in the Antarctic', *J Appl Ecol*, 3 (supplement) (1966), 155–67

45 Moore, N. W. and Tatton, J. O'G. 'Organochlorine residues in the eggs of seabirds', *Nature, Lond*, 207

46 Prestt, Ian and Jefferies, D. J. 'Winter Numbers, Breeding Success and Organochlorine Residues in the Great Crested Grebe in Britain', *Bird Study*, 16 (1969), 168–85

47 Prestt, Ian. 'Studies of Recent Changes in the Status of some Birds of Prey and Fish-feeding Birds in Britain', *J Appl Ecol*, 3 (supplement) (1966), 107–12

48 See the annual reports on deaths of birds and mammals from toxic chemicals issued annually, 1961–4 by the Joint Committee of the

British Trust for Ornithology and the Royal Society for the Protection of Birds, in collaboration with the Game Research Association.

49 The causal relationships are described in D. A. Ratcliffe's key paper: 'Changes Attributable to Pesticides in Egg Breakage Frequency and Eggshell Thickness in some British Birds', *J Appl Ecol*, 7 (1970), 67–115

50 See Ratcliffe, D. A. 'The Status of the Peregrine in Great Britain', *Bird Study*, 10 (1963), 56–90; Ratcliffe, D. A. 'The Peregrine Situation in Great Britain, 1963–4', *Bird Study*, 12 (1965), 66–82; Ratcliffe, D. A. 'The Peregrine Situation in Great Britain 1965–6', *Bird Study*, 14 (1967), 238–46; etc; Ian Prestt's enquiry into the status of the smaller birds of prey and crows (*Bird Study*, 12, 1965), first revealed the great extent of the sparrowhawk decline over the decade from 1953–63.

51 Lockie, J. D. and Ratcliffe, D. A. 'Insecticides and Scottish Golden Eagles', *Brit Birds*, 57 (1964), 89–102

52 See eg Lockie, J. D., Ratcliffe, D. A. and Balharry, R. 'Breeding success and Organochlorine Residues in Golden Eagles in West Scotland', *J Appl Ecol*, 6 (1969), 381–9

53 Ratcliffe, loc cit (1970)

54 Ratcliffe, loc cit (1965)

55 Tubbs, C. R. 'Analysis of Nest Record Cards for the Buzzard', *Bird Study*, 19 (1972), 96–104

56 Ratcliffe, loc cit (1970)

57 Mr P. A. Gouldsbury (Hon Secretary Gamekeepers' Association of the United Kingdom) in litt, 19 April 1971, agreed that there had been little change in the position since 1954, except that the number of keepers in Hampshire, Sussex and Lincolnshire had probably increased. Dr N. W. Moore's data for the distribution of gamekeepers in 1955 was derived largely from information provided by Major A. W. Neve, the then Hon Secretary of the Gamekeepers' Association. I am grateful to Pat Gouldsbury for bringing this information up to date.

58 See eg Conder, Peter. 'Pole Traps in Perspective', *Birds*, 3 (12) (1971), 294

59 Barber, Derek. 'Predators and Game Preservation', *Birds*, 3 (9) (1971), 209–10

60 Conder, loc cit

61 Tubbs, loc cit

62 Porter, R. F. (Technical Officer, RSPB) in litt

63 For a useful discussion of the population ecology of game-bird populations see: Murton, R. K. *Man and Birds* (1971), Chapter 3; for a general survey see: Watson, Adam. 'Animal Population Ecology', *Sci Prog Oxf*, 59, 451–74
64 Curry-Lindahl, Kai. 'Conservation and Predation Problems of Birds of prey in Sweden', *Brit Birds*, 54 (1961), 297–306
65 Rudebeck, G. 'The Choice of Prey and Modes of Hunting by Predatory Birds, with Special Reference to their Selective Effect', *Oikos*, 2 (1950–1), 65–88, 200–31

Chapter Four *Social Behaviour* (pages 92–121)

1 The scientific importance and management history of the New Forest are described in: Tubbs, C. R. *The New Forest: An Ecological History*, Newton Abbot (1969)
2 Dare, P. J. *Ecological Observations on a Breeding Population of Common Buzzards* Buteo buteo (*L.*) *with Particular Reference to the Diet and Feeding Habits*, PHD thesis, unpublished, Exeter University (1961)
3 Holdsworth, Michael. 'Breeding Biology of Buzzards at Sedbergh during 1937–67', *Brit Birds*, 64 (1971), 412–20
4 Warncke, Klaus and Wittenberg, Jochen. 'Uber Seidlungsdichte und Brutbiologie des Mäusebussards', *Vogelwelt*, 80 (1969), 101–8; Wendland, Victor. 'Populationsstudien auf Raubvogeln', *J Orn*, 93 (1952), 144–53
5 Melde, M. 'Das Revier des Mäusebussards', *Falke*, 7 (1960), 100–5
6 Thiollay, Jean-Marc. 'Ecologie d'une population de rapaces diurnes en Lorraine', *La Terre et la Vie*, 2 (1967), 116–95

Chapter Five *Breeding Biology* (pages 122–151)

1 See eg: Seidensticker, John C. and Reynolds, Harry V. 'The Nesting, Reproductive Performance and Chlorinated Hydrocarbon Residues in the Red-tailed Hawk and Great Horned Owl in South-central Montana', *The Wilson Bulletin*, 83 (1971), 408–18; Seidensticker, John C. 'Food of Nesting Red-tailed Hawks in South-central Montana', *The Murrelet*, 51 (1970), 38–40
2 Tubbs, C. R. 'Analysis of Nest Record Cards for the Buzzard', *Bird Study*, 19 (1972), 96–104
3 Weinzel, Frank. *The Buzzard* (1959)

4 Dare, P. J. *Ecological Observations on a Breeding Population of Common Buzzards* Buteo buteo (*L.*) . . ., PHD thesis, unpublished, Exeter University (1961)

5 Davis, T. A. W. and Saunders, D. R. 'Buzzards on Skomer Island', *Nature in Wales*, 9 (1965), 116–24

6 Holdsworth, Michael. 'Breeding Biology of Buzzards at Sedbergh during 1937–67', *Brit Birds*, 64 (1971), 412–20

7 Table 3 is reproduced from Tubbs, loc cit, with the permission of the British Trust for Ornithology.

8 See eg: Mebs, T. 'Zur Biologie und Populationsdynamik des Mäussebussards (*Buteo buteo*)', *J Orn*, 105 (1964), 247–306

9 Witherby, H. F., Jourdain, F. C. R., Ticehurst, N. F. and Tucker, B. W. *The Handbook of British Birds*, V (1949), Supplementary Additions and Corrections, 296

10 *Brit Birds*, 39 (1946), 346; 40 (1947), 182–3; 41 (1948), 53–4; Dare, op cit; Holdsworth, loc cit

11 Witherby, Jourdain, Ticehurst and Tucker, op cit

12 Panting, P. J. in litt (1965)

13 MacNally, L. 'Food at a Buzzard's Nest', *Scottish Birds*, 2 (1962), 196–8

14 Lockie, J. D. 'The Breeding and Feeding of Jackdaws and Rooks with Notes on Carrion Crows and other Corvidae', *Ibis*, 97 (1955), 341–69. See also: Lack, D. *The Natural Regulation of Animal Numbers*, Oxford (1954)

15 Curry-Lindahl, Kai. 'Conservation and Predation Problems of Birds of Prey in Sweden', *Brit Birds*, 54 (1961), 297–306

16 Uttendörfer, O. *Neue Ergebnisse über die Ernahrung der Greifvögel und Eulen*, Stuttgart (1952)

17 Craighead, J. J. and Craighead, F. C. *Hawks, Owls and Wildlife*, Stockpole Co, Harrisburg, Penn, and Wildlife Management Institute, Washington DC (1956)

Chapter Six *Population Ecology* (pages 152–178)

1 Tubbs, C. R. 'Analysis of Nest Record Cards for the Buzzard', *Bird Study*, 19 (1972), 96–104

2 Davis, T. A. W. and Saunders, D. R. 'Buzzards on Skomer Island, 1954–64', *Nature in Wales*, 9 (1965), 116–24

3 Holdsworth, Michael. 'Breeding Biology of Buzzards at Sedbergh during 1937–67', *Brit Birds*, 64 (1971), 412–20

4 Holstein, V. *Musvaagen*, Buteo buteo buteo (*L.*), Copenhagen (1956)

5 Warncke, Klaus and Wittenberg, Jochen. 'Uber Siedlungsdichte und Brutbiologie des Mäusebussards (*Buteo buteo*)', *Vogelwelt*, 80 (1959), 101–8

6 Mebs, T. 'Zur Biologie und Populationsdynamik des Mäusebussards (*Buteo buteo*)', *J Orn*, 105 (1964), 247–306

7 Wendland, Victor. 'Populationsstudien aut Raubvogeln—I. Zur Vermehrung des Mäusebussards (*Buteo b. buteo* (*L.*))', *J Orn*, 93 (1952), 144–53

8 Dare, P. J. *Ecological Observations on a Breeding Population of Common Buzzards,* Buteo buteo (*L.*) *with Particular Reference to the Diet and Feeding Habits,* PHD thesis, unpublished, Exeter University (1961)

9 *Per* Hon D. N. Weir

10 Holdsworth, loc cit

11 Davis and Saunders, loc cit

12 *Per* Mr Shaun White (RSPB Warden, Ramsey)

13 Breeding data for 1972 became available shortly after completion of the book. No complete census of the population was possible but breeding or attempted breeding was recorded for 18 territories. In 2 nests the eggs failed to hatch. From the remaining 16 nests 22 young flew, giving an average of 1.2 per nest or 1.4 per successful nest. These results are similar to those obtained during 1962–71 and in no way affect conclusions drawn in the text. It is of interest that the nest in territory 6, which had already been occupied for at least thirteen consecutive years, was again in use—though for the second year running the eggs failed to hatch, suggesting perhaps the final onset of infertility.

14 I am indebted to the late Mr Oliver Hook for the data in Table 9.

15 Weir, D. N. and Picozzi, N. 'Work on Buzzards', *Research on Vertebrate Predators in Scotland, Progress Report, 1970,* The Nature Conservancy (1970)

16 Olsson, Viking. 'Dispersal, Migration, Longevity and Death causes of *Strix aluco, Buteo buteo, Ardea cinerea* and *Larus argentatus*', *Acta Vertebratica,* 1 (2) (1958), 91–189

17 Mayard, Noel. 'Coup d'oeil sur les reprises en France de Buses variables *Buteo buteo*', *Alauda,* 23 (1955), 225–48

18 Kuhk, R. 'Mäusebussards (*Buteo b. buteo*) von 19 und fast 24 jahren', *Vogelwelt*, 16 (1952), 123

19 Barber, Derek. 'More Hawks for the People', *New Scientist* (27 April 1972), 212–13

INDEX

This index is to the body of the text: it does not cover the Appendix or the Notes and References. Names of authors mentioned in the text are also omitted.